LIVING FROM THE HEART

GANDHI'S DISCOURSES ON THE GITA

First Edition, December 1985

ACKNOWLEDGEMENTS

Gandhi's **Discourses on the Gita** are reprinted here with the gracious permission of the Navajivan Trust, Ahmedabad, India. 25% of the net profits received from this book will go to the Trust, established by Gandhi for the benefit of *Harijans* (the downtrodden) of India.

Thanks: to the Navajivan Trust; to the library of the Resource Center for Nonviolence in Santa Cruz for their wonderful work and their kind assistance to me; to the following people for their support and helpful feedback—Umesh Jain, Diana Wachner, Linda Peluso, Billy Ray Boyd, Gina Ryerson, Beth Abrams, Tom Taber, Paul Quinlan, Clay Olson, Linda Van Poppelen (and others at BookCrafters), Margie Shinnick, and my parents; to Richard Attenborough for having made the film "Gandhi".

Table of Contents

LIVING FROM THE HEART

Introduction

A WORD ABOUT THIS BOOK

It is with great pleasure that I reprint here an English translation of Gandhi's marvellous **Discourses on the Gita,** together with some explanatory and background remarks. This book is for anyone, whether or not familiar with the *Bhagavad Gita* or with Gandhi. The Gita deals with key issues that everybody faces in life. In addition to presenting powerful philosophical, religious and psychological insights, it is also of immense **practical value.** It is for all of us who wish to build more fully into our own lives the kind of self-discipline, compassion, strength, and inner satisfaction that Gandhi had developed in himself to such a remarkable degree.

A WORD ABOUT GANDHI

Mohandas K. Gandhi (known as "Mahatma") was a rather extraordinary individual. Now, with the release of the wonderful film biography by Richard Attenborough, most Americans are now aware of him and something of his accomplishments.

By his own account much a failure in early life, Gandhi left India as a young man to establish himself as a lawyer in South Africa. We get a picture of him at this time as an excruciatingly shy, rather fussy individual, a domineering, sexually driven husband (he was married at 13, by a family arrangement according to Indian custom), crudely attempting to ape the life of the British gentry. (He even wore spats and took violin lessons!)

Gandhi had barely arrived there when he was booted off a train for refusing to give up his first class compartment, from which "coloreds" were excluded. The unknowing railway conductor thus catapulted this odd young man not only onto the station platform, but also into a quite successful human rights career.

Gandhi promptly blossomed into a talented and effective activist. He had personal charisma, was an indefatiguable organizer, and spoke eloquently. After impressive victories in South Africa he returned home to rapidly become the central leader of millions in the Indian independence movement, which, under his influence, succeeded in nonviolently extricating the British colonists and in implementing many economic improvements at the village level throughout India, though it meant him spending roughly one-sixth of his long life in prison at various times for nonviolent civil disobedience.

But beyond these biographical items, Gandhi remains fascinating to us as well for being the sort of person he was. He was able to impress almost everyone with whom he came in contact, ally or adversary, by his warmth, integrity, devotion to service, and inspiring personality. Very much a lovable character, people everywhere showered him with affection and called him by nicknames, first "brother" (*bhai*) and then "Father" (*bapu*). He eventually became known as *Mahatma* (a title given to a very few spiritually advanced individuals meaning "Great Soul"). But even as Mahatma, people called him "Gandhiji", an affectionate familiar form in India.

He managed to treat everyone with genuine courtesy and respect, including those who perpetrated the degrading or atrocious acts he fought against. He lived precisely as he believed, and as he advised others to do. Gradually over time he adopted and refined a simple, basic lifestyle, divesting himself of possessions, freeing himself from sensory pleasures, including giving up foods for the palate (eating instead only to fuel his body), and even becoming celibate, all to purify himself body and soul so that he could be more connected to what he considered important in life.

Gandhi was meticulously honest and true to his word. In fact, truth was so important that he named the central principle of his method for nonviolent social change "Truth Force" [*Satyagraha*, also referred to as "Soul Force"], and eventually decided that, literally, "Truth is God". Yet he balanced his fanatical adherence to Truth with an openmindedness according to which he refused to impose his particular version of truth upon anyone else.

Gandhi had immense compassion for the misfortunate, a huge capacity to act effectively on their behalf, and a knack for inspiring others to do the same. Though often in extremely harrowing and highly emotionally charged situations, he never seemed to lose his composure, or let the zealous admiration of millions go to his head.

Together with all this, Gandhi's great love for people and life simply beamed out from him wherever he went. He was thoroughly nonviolent, fearless and direct, even in life-threatening situations. He was tough and persistent, sometimes exasperatingly so to his colleagues and certainly to his adversaries. Yet despite the pressures of his position and the horrors with which he came in contact, he generally remained cheery and optimistic, consistently working 18 to 20 hour days for years at a stretch and maintaining a lively sense of humor throughout it all.

Gandhi also managed to live as a devoutly religious Hindu while at the same time espousing that all major religions are equally valid, being merely different paths to the same goal.

But perhaps this description sounds too good to be true. Certainly those of us who are partial to Gandhi must avoid romanticizing, mythifying, or cultifying him, as many have done, or of being blind to his faults, which he certainly had. He was considered by many to be manipulative and domineering (despite his claim of being non-coercive), and fanatically obsessed with having his own way. He had problems in his own family — his eldest son rebelled against him, took to sensuality and materialism, published a scathing attack on his father, and there never was a reconciliation. Erik Erikson, in his wonderful book **Gandhi's Truth**, makes a good case that one incident where Gandhi claims to have been "at death's door" from having carried out a vow to eschew milk, was in actuality a nervous breakdown. And so on.

But Gandhi himself constantly talked about his fallibility and inadequacies. And even though his admirers can get carried away, the basic picture of Gandhi as an extremely gifted and inspiring person is simply too well documented by too many diverse sources not to be accurate.

He was, in fact, such a stunning example of what a human being can be like, that it's a little intimidating for the rest of us. Yet he thought of himself as a completely ordinary person, with no special talents, who simply chose the right path. He also believed that any individual could acquire the same abilities and accomplish the same things, if only that person made equally determined efforts. And he happily invites us to try.

Of course who knows how much of Gandhi's extraordinary abilities can be ascribed to his own unique constellation of qualities and talents, how much to the particular circumstances of his life, times, and culture, and how much to a chosen method of living that anyone can follow. But, however we decide to sort that out, his assertion that any of us can achieve similar results is certainly worth exploring.

And if we are to accept Gandhi's invitation — to take the principles he found so helpful and turn them however best we can to good advantage in our own lives — then one place to start is by examining his chosen guidebook to life, the *Bhagavad Gita*.

The relation of the Gita to Gandhi's life is best expressed by Gandhi himself:

> "... to me the Gita became an infallible guide of conduct. It became my dictionary of daily reference. Just as I turned to the English dictionary for the meanings of English words that I did not understand, I turned to this dictionary of conduct for a ready solution of all my troubles and trials."

> "I have, for years past, been swearing by the Bhagavadgita, and have said that it answers all my difficulties and has been my *Kamadhenu*, my guide, my open sesame, on hundreds of moments of doubt and diffi-

> culty. I cannot recall a single occasion when it has failed me."
>
> "The Gita inculcates upon [all] the duty of perseverance in the face of seeming failure. It teaches us that we have a right to actions only but not to the fruit thereof and that success and failure are one and the same thing at bottom. It calls upon us to dedicate ourselves, body, mind and soul, to pure duty, and not to become mental voluptuaries at the mercy of all chance desires and undisciplined impulses."
>
> "... I must confess to you that when doubts haunt me, when disappointments stare me in the face, and when I see not one ray of light on the horizon I turn to the Bhagavadgita and find a verse to comfort me; and I immediately begin to smile in the midst of overwhelming sorrow. My life has been full of external tragedies and if they have not left any visible and indelible effect on me, I owe it to the teaching of the Bhagavadgita."

THE GITA AS 'RELIGIOUS'

The *Bhagavad Gita* is a book from the Hindu scriptures, written around 500 B.C. in Sanskrit. It is a deeply philosophical work dealing foremostly with religious ideas. However, its penetrating analysis of human psychology (and also of natural law) extends to many other dimensions as well. The Gita, despite its Hindu origin, applies to people of all religions, and depends in no way on the pre-acceptance of any specific religious belief. Even those readers (such as myself) who are not especially 'religion-oriented' should not be put off by the Gita's religious cast and terminology, for it speaks with equal clarity and force to us as well.

"God" is seen not only as sacred and divine, an object of worship, but also as a 'summary' of all phenomena in the universe, a distillation or embodiment of **principles** underlying natural law. Gandhi himself said:

> "I do not regard God as a person. Truth for me is God, and God's Law and God are not different things or facts, in the sense that an earthly [ruler] and [that ruler's] law are different. Because God is an Idea, Law [it]self. Therefore it is impossible to conceive God as breaking the Law. [God] therefore does not rule our actions and withdraw .... When we say [God] rules our actions, we are simply using human language and we try to limit [God]. Otherwise [God] and [God's] Law abide everywhere and govern everything."

"Attaining union with God", the Gita's central theme, is not merely a religious formula; it is also a sophisticated human life process based on a perceptive, mature, intelligent understanding of human nature. The Gita's advice to follow the path of discipline and devotion is not blind exhortation, but cogently reasoned argument combined with common sense and an appeal to experience. Even reincarnation, something not all of us accept literally, can be interpreted as referring broadly to the many cyclic patterns in our lives.

In general, the Gita, to the extent there is in it something universally true, must make sense to us not merely when viewed as a religious text, or as Hindu scripture, or as ancient Indian literature; it must make sense as a document before us here and now, to be examined with critical intelligence, bearing a direct relation to our lives and experiences at this time and in our society.

THE GITA - MAKING IT EASIER TO APPROACH

Because the Gita is an ancient text originating in a foreign culture and written in a foreign tongue, it is not the most approachable work for Westerners. Also, it is itself only a chapter in a much larger work, a huge epic story called the *Mahabharata*, and thus begins in the middle.

My own first bout with the Gita was a failure. After trudging through two pages of unpronounceable words ("*Dhritarashtra*", "*Kurukshetra*", "*Duryodhana*", etc.), I simply gave up. It was only after considerable exposure to material by and about Gandhi that I was inspired to try again, this time with success. Hopefully, first-timers will here be spared a similar discouraging experience as I had. In fact, Gandhi's **Discourses on the Gita** — chapter-by-chapter paraphrasings, with comments and explanations added — are themselves written in straightforward language (for the ordinary Indian villager), precisely to make its message plain to those for whom it would otherwise be buried in scholarly jargon. Though not meant to be in any sense a substitute for the Gita, these **Discourses** nonetheless can stand on their own. Furthermore, because of their relative clarity and simplicity, they are likely to constitute an easier and more direct **initial** route through which a Westerner can approach the Gita (and the inner workings of Gandhi), than that of reading the Gita itself. [For those interested at any point to read (or re-read) the Gita, I recommend Eknath Easwaran's marvellous English translation-with-commentary, **The Bhagavad Gita for Daily Living,** in 3 volumes, Nilgiri Press, Box 477, Petaluma, California 94953.]

Like the Christian Bible and other religious works, the Gita has been the subject of many heated and personal interpretations. Gandhi's view, represented here in his **Discourses,** differs from that of many other Hindus. The view contained in my added notes differs as well from his. The Gita is, furthermore, a sacred and divine book to millions of people across the world now as it has been throughout centuries. So, as a non-Hindu I make this undertaking into controversial matters outside my own religious background in a spirit of admiration and respect, and with the hope that I will not have trampled at all upon the sensibilities of any individual, Hindu or otherwise, for whom such issues are so close to the heart.

THE GITA - THE BASIC STORY

As mentioned above, the Gita constitutes but one brief interlude in a grand, lengthy epic story, the *Mahabharata*. And, though it's not necessary for one to know the *Mahabharata* in detail in order to understand the message of the Gita, it's nonetheless worth a few words of explanation now to make the Discourse on Chapter 1 which follows more readily understandable. (Throughout this book I adopt the policy of using the **minimum** number of Hindu names and special terms needed to convey the essential meaning of the **Discourses.**)

As the Gita opens, the central character of the *Mahabharata*, Arjuna, is about to lead the army of his family, of which he is commanding general, into battle. Arjuna — a hardened soldier — is tough, brave, honorable, practical, and at the same time possessed of a very strong moral sense. So in many ways he fits the role of the inspiring hero of a grand epic drama. However, his character has another side as well, according to which he is basically like you or me, just an ordinary person, with ordinary feelings and attachments, caught in and wrestling with the powerful forces of life. Arjuna's opponent in battle is a rival family, though one with which he was, in the past, quite close. According to the story, Arjuna's side is clearly in the right, and the other in the wrong.

So, we encounter the main figure of this drama facing an enemy on the battlefield in a just cause, all his soldiers in formation, primed and ready to fight. In fact, the battle is just moments away from starting, with the troops merely awaiting his command to attack. But Arjuna, in full regalia and battle gear, standing proud in his chariot, holds off for a moment from giving the order, and instead asks his charioteer, Krishna, to pull them up to a spot between the two armies so he can get a view of the entire area. (The battlefield area is called *Kurukshetra*. Krishna is also called Shri Krishna, "Shri" a title meaning "Lord". Arjuna's family are the *Pandavas*; his rivals are the *Kauravas*.)

When they arrive at that vantage point, Arjuna, after making estimates of the size and strength of his opponents, peers into the enemy ranks. He observes within them people he has known all his life. Some are old friends; some are gifted and respected teachers who meant a lot to Arjuna when he was growing up. Others are relatives with whom he feels the bonds of family. Seeing them now, spread out before him, about to be slaughtered by his own army, Arjuna suddenly realizes the full implications of what he is doing, and feels trapped.

On the one hand, he is committed to fighting. He knows his side is right; he knows the other side is the aggressor and must be stopped, and that he must defend his family or they will be annihilated. But, on the other hand, the thought of slaughtering loved ones and respected friends is completely intolerable. So, bitterly torn, shaking with emotion, Arjuna breaks down and pours out his feelings to Krishna.

Now, you must understand that Krishna is not merely Arjuna's charioteer, and his friend; he happens also to be a manifestation of God in human form.

Thus it is at that juncture that Arjuna, presented with this agonizing dilemma, learns, directly from the highest source, those principles of understanding and action which will resolve his crisis and as well reveal a method of living that offers to extricate him (and us) from those tenacious patterns of behavior in which we are caught and through which we bring ourselves to grief.

It is this advice given by Krishna to Arjuna that contains the germ and soul of the *Bhagavad Gita*. Gandhi felt its message and strove untiringly every moment of his life (with considerable success) to become a living embodiment of it. He attempted through the **Discourses** (as supplementary to his actions and life), to convey as clearly and directly as possible, in plain unadorned language, how he understood what the Gita was trying to tell us.

A WORD ABOUT THIS EDITION

I reprint these **Discourses** as translated into English (from Gujurati) by Mr. Valgi G. Desai as they appear in **In Search of the Supreme**, Volume III, edited by V. B.

Kher, Navajivan Press, India. The only changes I introduce are to substitute non-male-emphasized expressions for "he", "him", "his", and the like, when men and women collectively are being referred to. I do this because the Gita applies equally to women as to men, and because I believe the masculine emphasis to be (unintendedly) prejudicial against women. (Gandhi, a strong supporter of women's equality, probably would not object to such alterations to his work.) I didn't bother to document these numerous adjustments, but those with concerns about this are invited to compare my version with its source. Also, those few quotations appearing in the original Sanskrit language were not reproduced here.

I embedded V. B. Kher's footnotes (which were always brief) directly into the appropriate place in the main text of the **Discourses.** Those remarks of V. G. Desai occurring within that text appear as well in this edition, also in parentheses. Parenthesized material is Kher's unless marked "*Trans*" or initialled "V.G.D.".

Desai's "Translator's Notes" appear here in a separate chapter, just as they do in **In Search of the Supreme.** Supplementary notes authored by myself are appended to their respective Discourses. These notes are clearly indented, each preceded by a short re-quote of the Discourse material to which it refers. All additions to the text by me (supplementary notes, minor corrections, etc.) at any place past this introductory chapter are set in brackets.

Aside from those discussed above, no other rearrangements or alterations to the **Discourses** were performed.

My supplementary comments were added for two purposes. Firstly, they propose alternative interpretations of Gita/Discourse passages which are less literal and more compatible with the philosophical/religious background of the modern Western reader. And, secondly, they attempt to identify and discuss some perplexing and paradoxical aspects of the Gita's message. These comments of course represent my own point of view, which does not necessarily correspond to that of Gandhi. For reasons of space, they address only a few of the many issues covered or alluded to in the **Discourses.** Furthermore, they do not explain every term and name, only those (not otherwise explained) which seemed to be essential to a basic understanding of the text. I urge the reader not to balk at an unfamiliar word or get held up over details, and to seek out additional reading material for further background and information.

The reprint of Gandhi's **Discourses** you now hold is not primarily for the purpose of increasing academic or intellectual knowledge, for achieving certain 'spiritual experiences', nor even to convey insights. Rather, it is meant as a practical and direct aid toward leading a better life. Gandhi had no sympathy for armchair morality. The whole reason for reading the Gita, or about it, is to transform oneself **through action.** So, it is not over when you have finished reading the words and turning the pages. The true results are to be seen in changes in you as a person, in how you treat others, and, overall, in how you lead your life.

A. Saluk
San Francisco, California
August 24, 1985

DISCOURSES ON GITA

(The following are a series of letters written to Sabarmati Ashram inmates by Gandhiji during his incarceration in Yeravda Prison following the historic Dandi March in 1930. They have been translated into English from Gujarati by Mr. Valji G. Desai.)

DISCOURSE ON CHAPTER I

When the Pandavas and the Kauravas gathered together on the battle-field of Kurukshetra (the field of Kuru) with their armies, Duryodhana the king of Kauravas, approached Drona (his teacher in the science of war) and named the leading warriors on either side. As a signal for the battle to begin, conch-shell horns were sounded on both sides and Shri Krishna who was Arjuna's charioteer drove his chariot into a place between the two armies. The scene which greeted Arjuna's eyes unnerved him, and he said to Shri Krishna, 'How can I attack these in battle? I might fight readily enough if I had to fight with strangers, but these are my kin. The Kauravas and that Pandavas are first cousins. We were brought up together. Drona is our teacher as well as of the Kauravas'. Bhishma is a revered elder for both. How can I fight with him? It is true that the Kauravas are criminals and doers of evil deeds. They have wronged the Pandavas and deprived them of their lands. They have insulted the saintly Draupadi. But what shall I gain by killing them? They are fools indeed. But shall I also be equally foolish? I have some little knowledge. I can discriminate between right and wrong. I thus see that it is a sin to fight with relatives. Never mind if they have taken wrongful possession of the Pandavas' share in the kingdom. Never mind even if they kill us. But how dare we raise our hand against them? O Krishna, I will not fight with my kith and kin.'

With these words, Arjuna sank down on the seat of the chariot, being overwhelmed by grief.

Here ends the first Chapter which is entitled 'the sorrow of Arjuna'. All of us should feel pain even as Arjuna did. No acquisition of knowledge is possible unless there is in us a sense of something lacking and a desire to know the truth. If one is not curious even to know what is wrong and what is right, what is the use of religion for such a person? The battle-field of Kurukshetra only provides the occasion for the dialogue between Arjuna and Krishna. The real Kurukshetra is the human heart, which is also a *dharmakshetra* (the field of righteousness) if we look upon it as the abode of God and invite God to take hold of it. Some battle or other is fought on this battle-field from day to day. Most of these battles arise from the distinction between 'mine' and 'thine', between kin and strangers. Therefore, as we shall find later on, the Lord tells Arjuna that attraction (*raga*) and repulsion (*dvesha*) lie at the root of sin. When I look upon a person or thing as 'mine', *raga* takes hold of my mind; and when I look upon a person as a stranger, aversion or hatred enters the mind. Therefore we must forget the distinction between 'mine' and 'thine'. That is to say, we must give up our likes and dislikes. This is the teaching of the Gita and all other scriptures. To say this is one thing; to practise it is quite another. The Gita is there to teach us how to practise it. We will try to understand the method it recommends.

Supplementary Notes to Gandhi's Discourse I

"Attraction and repulsion lie at the root of sin"

> [This is a main theme of the Gita, that the sensory world of likes, dislikes, attractions, repulsions, lusts, anger, and so forth, makes a very loud noise in our ears, but actually hides a more satisfactory and enduring reality underlying it. A word like "sin" can be taken in a general sense, to mean what is counterproductive in life, in addition to our typical associations of the word of doing 'evil' things.]

"Therefore we must forget the distinction between 'mine' and 'thine'. That is to say, we must give up our likes and dislikes."

[This is the idea of selflessness, or non-ego. If we are possessive of ourselves or of what we have control over, then the world becomes partitioned into 'ours' vs. 'theirs'. (This includes the emotional and interpersonal as well as the material.) Operating within such a framework, we feel driven to protect and build up our 'domain', if necessary at the expense of others, in order to be safe and fulfilled. We are thereby more likely to get caught up in being defensive or angry and lock into a system of separateness and hostility towards those we dislike.

This self-centered framework can be contrasted with an egoless one, in which we perceive ourselves and others as being interlinked, all in the same boat, a mutual part of a grander system. Egoless, we strive to see ourselves in others and others in ourselves.

By not being possessive, by not staking a claim to territory exclusively for ourselves, we become less threatening to others; we have no need of their 'territory'. By not burdening ourselves with unnecessary acquisitions, we are less threatened by others, since we have less in our exclusive possession to 'lose' to them. As a result, we can melt those structures of feeling and reaction within us which predispose to defensiveness, fear, anger, and hate, and which touch off those responses in others.

This does not mean being patronizingly nice to those we dislike. Nor does it mean denying the reality of others' attempts in this world to take advantage of us, or allowing ourselves to be taken advantage of. It merely means removing our possessiveness, acquisitiveness, and defensiveness when dealing with the rest of the world. It means getting beyond our reactions of liking or disliking someone — of being threatened by or feeling the need to be threatening towards someone and instead to keep our hearts as open as possible. Only when this principle is actually put into practice do we begin to realize how much worthwhile in the world we shut out and how many antagonisms we ourselves create or perpetuate as a result of a possessive attitude.]

DISCOURSE ON CHAPTER II

When Arjuna had picked himself [up] a little bit, the Lord rebuked him and said, 'How is it that this delusion has come to you? It is unworthy of a warrior like you.' But even then Arjuna stuck to his first position, refused to fight and said, 'If in order to get it, I have to slay elders and other relations, I do not want not only a kingdom on this earth but even the delights of paradise. My mind gropes in darkness. I do not know where my duty lies. I put myself into your hands. Please guide me.'

Finding that Arjuna was bewildered and aspired after knowledge, Krishna had pity on him and proceeded to explain things to him: 'Your sorrow is for nothing, and you utter words about wisdom without understanding. You have evidently forgotten the distinction between the body and the embodied soul. The soul never dies; but the body passes through childhood, youth and age and perishes in the end. The body is born but the soul is birthless and unchanging. It ever was, is now and will be there for all time to come. For whom then do you grieve? Your grief arises from a delusion. You look upon these Kauravas as your own, but you are aware that their bodies will come to an end. And as for the souls which inhabit these bodies, no one can destroy them. The soul cannot be wounded by weapons, burned by fire, dried by the wind or drowned in water. Then again, consider this from the standpoint of your duty as a warrior with an army under your command. If you refuse to fight this righteous war, the consequences will be the very reverse of what you expect and you will become an object of ridicule. You have always enjoyed the reputation of being brave. But if now you withdraw from the battle, you will be supposed to have been driven from it by fear. If it were part of your duty to flee in the face of danger, disgrace would not matter, but if you retire from battle now, you will have failed to discharge your duty, and people will be justified in condemning your flight.

'Thus far, I have tried to reason out things, draw a distinction between the body and the soul and remind you of your duty as a warrior. But let me now explain the

Karmayoga (the method of action). A practitioner of Karmayoga never comes to harm. It has nothing to do with chopping logic. It is something to be translated into action and experience. An ounce of practice is more profitable than tons of argumentation. And this practice too must not be vitiated by speculation about its fruit. Literalists perform Vedic rites directed to the acquisition of material rewards. If one rite does not yield the expected fruit, they have recourse to another, and being disappointed once more, they take up a third. And thus they suffer from utter mental confusion. As a matter of fact, it is up to us to do our duty without wasting a single thought on the fruits of our action. To fight is the duty you have to discharge at present. Gain or loss, defeat or victory, is not in your power. Why should you carry the needless burden of thinking about them and be like the dog who walks under a cart and imagines that it is being drawn by itself and not by the bullocks? Defeat and victory, heat and cold, pleasure and pain come to someone in turn and that person must put up with them. Without worrying about the fruit of action, an individual must be devoted to the performance of duty with an evenness of temper. This is yoga, or skill in action. The success of an act lies in performing it, and not in its result, whatever it is. Therefore be calm and do your duty clear of consequences.'

On hearing all this Arjuna said, 'The course of conduct you have mapped for me seems to be beyond my capacity. Not to worry about defeat or victory, not to waste a thought on the result, — how can one attain such an evenness of temper and steadfastness in spirit? How does someone with such attainments behave, and how are we to recognize such a person?'

The Lord replied, 'O king, one who renounces all the cravings which torment the heart and derives contentment from within is said to be a *sthitaprajna* or *samadhistha* (one stable in spirit). Such a person is unruffled in adversity, and does not hanker after happiness. Pleasure and pain are felt through the five senses. Therefore this wise individual draws the senses away from sense objects even as a tortoise draws in its limbs. The tortoise withdraws into its shell when it apprehends danger. But in the case of human beings sense objects are ready to attack the senses at all times; therefore their senses must always be drawn in, and they should be ever ready to fight against sense objects. This is the real battle. Some people resort to self-mortification and fasting as weapons of defence against sense objects. These measures have their limited use. The senses do not make for sense objects so long as a person is fasting, but fasting alone does not destroy one's relish for them. On the other hand that relish may be heightened when the fast is broken, and a person can get rid of it only with the grace of God. The senses are so powerful that they drag someone behind them by force if that person is not on guard. Therefore you must always keep them under control. This end can be achieved only if one turns one's eyes inward, realizes God Who resides in the heart, and is devoted to this God. If you thus look upon Me as your goal and surrender everything to Me, keeping the senses in control, you will be a yogi stable in spirit. On the other hand if you are not master of your senses, you will be always musing on the objects of sense and will conceive an attachment for them, so that you can hardly think of anything else. From this attachment will arise desire; and when the desire is thwarted you will get angry. Anger will drive you nearly mad. You won't be able to understand what you are about. You thus will lose your memory, behave in a disorderly manner and come to an ignoble end. When your senses rove at will, you are like a rudderless ship which is at the mercy of the gale and is broken to pieces on the rocks. People should therefore abandon all desires and restrain their senses, so that these do not indulge in undesirable activity. The eyes then will look straight and that too only at holy objects; the ears will listen to hymns in praise of God or to cries of distress; hands and feet will be engaged in service. Indeed all the organs of sense and of action will be employed in helping you to do your duty and making you a fit recipient of the grace of God. And once the grace of God has descended upon you, all your sorrows are at an end. As snow melts in the sunshine, all pain vanishes when the grace of God shines upon you and you are said to be stable in spirit. But if you are not stable-minded, how can you think good thoughts? Without good thoughts there is no peace, and without peace there is no happiness. Where a stable-minded individual sees things clear as daylight, the unstable person distracted by the turmoil of the world is as good as blind. On the other hand what is pure in the eyes of the worldly wise looks unclean to and repels the stable-minded individual. Rivers continuously flow into the sea, but the sea remains unmoved; in the same way all sense objects come to the yogi, but the yogi always remains calm like the sea. Thus one who abandons all desires, is free from pride and selfishness and behaves as one apart, finds peace. This is the condition of a perfect person of God, and any person who is established therein even at the final hour is saved (lit. set free, *mukta*).'

Supplementary Notes to Gandhi's Discourse II

"... their bodies will come to an end. And as for the souls which inhabit these bodies, no one can destroy them."

> [The 'soul' can be looked upon not as a separate entity outside of ordinary reality, but as a distillation of those aspects of reality which are permanent and enduring, as those real principles underlying and supervening particular events and occurrences. Although the Gita, and Gandhi, refer literally to the 'immortality of the soul', this can be interpreted more broadly as connection to or alignment with the stable, permanent aspects of life (versus the transient, unreliable world of our sensations). Those imperishable aspects of ourselves and of others will be there no matter what we do. The Gita is telling us not to be intimidated from pursuit of our ideal by the fear that we might disrupt anything of importance in our or others' lives.
>
> Literally the Gita is reassuring Arjuna that it's all right for him to slay his enemy, that he needn't worry about the killing that's involved, since it is the 'soul' that's

important and no one can harm that. However, this is the very opposite of what Gandhi, the apostle of nonviolence, would recommend!

Not to worry. Paradoxical as this may seem, Gandhi finds no true contradiction. For, according to him, the real battlefield of the Gita is the human heart, and the real enemy not the *Kauravas* but our own urgings and impulses.]

"it has nothing to do with chopping logic. It is something to be translated into action and experience."

[A constant theme with Gandhi. Don't waste too much time trying to logic everything out; you've got to get out there and actually change your life. Don't pour too much over books or intellectual exercise. 'Enlightenment' is not to be found there. Books will inspire you and point you in a general direction, but your true advancement is through action in the real world.

This admonition is not anti-intellectual. Your attitudes, understanding and life practice must all still survive the scrutiny of critical intelligence and logical consistency. However, the 'material' you are here dealing with is often more than the intellect can handle.

When in life we reach the limits of the availability or helpfulness of logic and scientific schema, we must look elsewhere to find a basis for decisions that have to be made. That does not mean that what we are then doing is unscientific or illogical.

Above all, we must not allow our inability to logic everything out in advance to immobilize us, to prevent us from doing what is necessary.

(NOTE: "Vedic rites" are Hindu religious rites/rituals. The *Vedas* are Hindu scriptures.)]

"it is up to us to do our duty without wasting a single thought on the fruits of our action."

[This is that method the Gita recommends with which Gandhi most closely identifies. Do what your heart tells you and don't worry about what happens from there. Don't work for results; work instead to carry out your proper obligations. The ultimate results of what you do are "in God's hands".

There is a certain common sense way in which this has truth; in that, no matter what you do, things will either go the way you hope or they won't, and there's no point to wasting energy in getting anxious over the outcome. You'll find out soon enough.

But the concept of laboring without concern for fruits goes beyond that. It proposes that we work 'with understanding' rather than for the purpose of accomplishing specific ends.

This idea sounds a little strange. How can anyone get motivated to do anything at all, if one isn't working for a result? The answer is that the true 'result' is in the action itself.

There's more about this later on in the Discourses.]

"evenness of temper"

[This also sounds odd; what's life without ups and downs? But I don't believe the Gita is advocating a bland life without any vividness or variety of experience. Rather, it's recommending one in which we steer clear of those ups and downs which catch us in self-defeating cycles, those attractions and aversions which hold us prisoner to grasping needs and dependencies — in short, those kinds of highs and lows which "bind us".

We are asked to be evenminded in the face of events that would otherwise pull us onto the sensory see-saw. These 'sensory' events include not only physical or bodily sensations, but also what attracts and repels us, what annoys, enrages, offends, or embarasses us, and so on. If we can patiently endure the siren calls of the sensory world by restraining our impulses to react, then we can escape entanglement, respond more appropriately, and mature into a better 'system' of operation. This is the way, the Gita says, to progress to a place 'closer to God', which is to say closer to our own true selves.]

"Pleasure and pain are felt through the five senses. Therefore this wise individual draws the senses away from sense objects ...."

[It's difficult to understand why we should be asked to avoid the pursuit of pleasure, but the Gita is persuasive in arguing that sensory gratification is not geniunely satisfying. According to the Gita (and Gandhi's life experience), the positive experience of sensory pleasure is miniscule in comparison to the effect achieved by living with disattachment. Even in the here-and-now, sensory pleasure contains much that is negative and depleting, though in our grasping attachment to the pleasurable part we blind ourselves to the rest.]

"The eyes then will look straight and that too only at holy objects; the ears will listen to hymns in praise of God or to cries of distress; hands and feet will be engaged in service."

[Except for the compassion/service part, this description of the religious life unfortunately is reminiscent of Mark Twain's satirical portrayal of Heaven (an extremely boring place). Nonetheless, there must be a lot of things in this world to which one can be properly and gratifyingly connected besides through singing religious hymns and gazing at 'holy objects'. What seems important here is not specific details of the 'religious' life, but rather the totality of the commitment that is involved in order to become a fulfilled human being, as well as the intensity of one's life experience after having achieved that condition.]

"... once the grace of God has descended upon you, all your sorrows are at an end."

[It is possible to think of "the grace of God" not so much as a miraculous gift from outside of yourself, a 'reward' for 'doing things right', but rather as the very nice thing that happens when, as a perfectly natural consequence of your disciplined, devoted actions and thoughts, you mature beyond the sensory level to a new and better way of functioning.]

DISCOURSE ON CHAPTER III

When Krishna had thus set forth the marks of identification for a *sthitaprajna* person, Arjuna received the impression that one had only to sit quiet in order to attain such a state, as Krishna had not made the slightest reference to any need for action on his part. He therefore asked Krishna, 'It seems as if you hold that knowledge is superior to action. If so, why are you urging me to this terrible deed and thus confusing my mind? Please tell me clearly where my welfare lies.'

Krishna replied: 'O sinless Arjuna, since the beginning of time seekers have taken one or the other of two different paths. In one of these the pride of place is given to knowledge and in the other it is given to action. But you will find that freedom from action cannot be attained without action, that wisdom never comes to someone simply on account of that person's having ceased to act. A person does not become perfect merely by renouncing everything. Don't you see that every one of us is doing something or other all the time? Our very nature impels us to action. Such being the law of nature, one who sits with folded hands but lets one's mind dwell on the objects of sense is a fool and may even be called a hypocrite. Rather than indulge in such senseless inactivity, is it not better that one should control the senses, overcome likes and dislikes, and engage in some activity or other without fuss and in a spirit of detachment? Do your allotted duty, restraining the organs of sense, for that is better than inaction. Idlers will only meet their end the sooner for their idleness. But while acting, remember that action leads to bondage unless it is performed in a spirit of sacrifice. Sacrifice (*yajna*) means exerting oneself for the benefit of others, in a word service. And where service is rendered for service's sake, there is no room for attachment, likes and dislikes. Perform such a sacrifice; render such service. When Brahma created the universe, Brahma created sacrifice along with it, as it were, and said to humankind, "Go forth into the world; serve one another and prosper. Look upon all creatures as gods. Serve and propitiate those gods, so that being pleased they will be gracious to you and fulfill your wishes unasked." Therefore understand that whoever enjoys the fruits of the earth, without serving the people and without having first given them their share, is a thief. And whosoever enjoys them after having given all creatures their share is entitled to such enjoyment and is thus freed from sin. On the other hand, those who labour only for themselves are sinners and eat the fruit of sin. It is a law of nature that creatures are sustained by food, food production depends on the rains, and the rains descend on the earth on account of *yajna*, that is to say, the labour of all creatures. There is no rain where there are no creatures, and it does rain where they are there. All live by labour; none can remain idle and live, and if this is true of the lower forms of life, it is still more applicable to humans. Action takes its origin from Brahma and Brahma from the imperishable *brahma*; therefore the imperishable *brahma* is present in all kinds of sacrifice or service. And whoever breaks this chain of mutual service is a sinner and lives in vain.

'When a person enjoys peace of mind and contentment, it may be said that there is nothing left for that person to do. Such an individual does not stand to gain by action or by inaction. This person has no personal interests to serve; and yet must not cease to offer sacrifice. Therefore do your duty from day to day without entertaining likes and dislikes and in a spirit of detachment. Whoever acts in such a spirit enjoys the beatific vision. Then again if even a selfless king like Janaka reached perfection all the while working for the good of the people, how can you behave in a way different from his? Whatever a good and great person does, common people imitate. Take My own case for instance. I have nothing to gain by action, and yet ceaselessly do I pour Myself in action. Hence it is that people too go on working more or less. But what would happen if I ceased to work? The world would collapse if the sun, the moon and the stars ceased to move. And it is I who set them in motion and regulate their activity. But there is a difference between My attitude and the attitude of the common person. I act in the spirit of perfect detachment while a common person harbours attachment and works in that person's own interest. If a wise person like you ceased to act, others too would do the same and their minds would be unsettled. Therefore do your duty without attachment, so that others might not cease to work and might gradually learn to work without attachment. A person is bound to work in obedience to and in conformity with that person's own nature. Only fools think that they themselves are the doers. To breathe is a part of a human being's nature; when an insect settles upon the eye, the eyelid moves of its own accord. And nobody says, "I take in the air" or "I move the eyelid". In the same manner why should not all human actions be performed in accordance with the qualities of nature? Why should there be any egoism about it? In order that someone may be able thus to act naturally and without attachment, the best thing for this person to do is to dedicate all actions to Me and perform them without egotism as a mere instrument in My hands. When you thus get over selfishness, all your actions are natural and free from taint and you escape many a trouble. Actions then have no binding force for you. Action being natural, it is sheer egoism to outrage nature and to claim to be inactive. The victim of such egoism will externally appear not to act, but this person's mind is always active in scheming. This is worse than external activity and has all the greater binding force.

'As a matter of fact the senses feel attraction and aversion for their respective objects. For instance the ears like to hear some things and do not like to hear other things. The nose likes to smell the rose, and does not like to smell dirt. This is also true of the other organs of sense. Therefore what each person has to do is not to submit to these two robbers, namely, attraction and repulsion. If one wishes to escape their attentions, one must not go about in search of action. One must not hanker after this today, that tomorrow and the other thing the day after. But one should hold oneself ready to render for the sake of God such service as falls to one's share. Thus you will cultivate within yourself the feeling that whatever you do is in fact an act of God and not your own, and your egoism will be a thing of the past. This is *svadharma* (one's own duty). Each individual must stick to *svadharma*, for it is the best for that person at any rate. *Paradharma* (another's duty) may appear to be better, but even so it should be looked upon as dangerous. *Moksha* (salvation) lies in embracing death while doing one's own duty.'

When Krishna said that action performed by one who is free from likes and dislikes is sacrifice, Arjuna asked, 'What is it that makes someone commit sin? Very often it seems as if one were driven to sin by some outsider against one's own will.'

Krishna replied: 'The slave drivers in this case are Kama (desire) and Krodha (anger). These are like blood relatives. If desire is not satisfied, anger is the inevitable consequence. One who is the slave of desire and anger is said to be inspired by *rajoguna* (the quality of passion), which is one's greatest enemy and against which one has to fight day in, day out. As dust hides a mirror, smoke suffocates a fire and the womb covers the embryo, even so anger deprives knowledge of its lustre and suffocates it. And desire is insatiable like fire, and taking possession of your senses, mind and intellect, knocks you down. Therefore first control your senses, and then conquer the mind. When you have done this, the intellect also will obey your orders. For though among the senses, the mind and the intellect, the mind is greater than the senses and the intellect is greater than the mind, the soul is the greatest of all. One has no idea of one's own strength or soul force, and tends to believe that the senses, the mind and the intellect are not amenable to one's control. But when once one has gained confidence in soul force, everything else becomes easy as a matter of course. And desire, anger and their countless hosts hold no terror for that person who has mastered the senses, the mind and the intelligence.'

I call this chapter the key to an understanding of the Gita, and the gist of it is that life is given us for service and not for enjoyment. We have therefore to impart a sacrificial character to our lives. Intellectual assent to this proposition is only the first step, but such assent and conduct in terms of that assent are bound to rid our heart of its impurities in course of time. But what is real service? In order to obtain the right answer to this question, restraint of the senses is essential, as it gives us a clearer and clearer vision of the God of truth. Service rendered with selfish motives ceases to be sacrifice. Hence the urgent need for the spirit of detachment. When this is understood, all manner of controversies lose their meaning for us. 'Did Krishna really ask Arjuna to kill his relatives? Could such killing even be a part of one's duty?' Questions like these are set at rest for ever. When detachment governs our actions, even the weapon raised in order to strike an enemy down falls out of our hand. But a mere pretence of detachment serves no useful purpose. If only we persevere in our effort, detachment may come to us, perhaps the very first day, or may be only after a thousand years. We must not worry over the time this takes, for the effort carries within itself the seeds of success. We must however be on our guard and make sure that it is a genuine effort, and that there is no self-deception. And this is certainly possible for us all.

Supplementary Notes to Gandhi's Discourse III

"action leads to bondage unless it is performed in a spirit of sacrifice[, which means] service."

> [If we do things for ourselves, we are in "bondage" to our self-interest and to our self-centeredness. If we do things for others, for the good of everything, then what happens to us personally, good or bad, doesn't matter so much. It's not that we are down on ourselves, or uncaring, just that if we merely 'send out' what we do without any further hopes or expectations of it, then what happens afterwards as a result is not our concern. The **doing** of it was what was important.
>
> We still need to be aware of and responsible for our actions, and we must still be capable of learning from our mistakes; but these things are separate from having anxiety about the future or regretting the past. And, after ridding ourselves of these anxieties, we are relaxed, and comfortable, released simply to be ourselves and do what's appropriate. How do we know what's appropriate? There is no single answer except to say that it becomes clearer to us as we emerge

from under the distorting filter of our neurotic attachments.

If we lose our ego, then what remains is the entire rest of the world. Being in service to that is being in harmony with everything else. 'Sacrifice' has connotations of pain and martyrdom, but what we are really being asked to sacrifice is the self-defeating system of self-preoccupation. To do this is initially painful, but ultimately satisfying.

One pitfall of devoting oneself entirely to the service of others is that tendency to neglect or punish oneself, or else to use 'service' as an excuse to avoid being assertive. This idea of the fearful or passive avoidance of self-assertion using 'service' or 'nonviolence' as an excuse was anathema to Gandhi. He often stated that he preferred even violence to fear-ridden passivity. Nonetheless, the balance between selflessness and assertiveness is a difficult one to attain.]

"dedicate all ... actions to Me and perform them without egoism as a mere instrument in My hands."

[The surrender of our ego to the world at large, discarding our possessiveness and self-interest, can be called 'being an instrument of God'.]

"[Rendering service for the sake of God] will cultivate within ... the feeling that whatever you do is in fact an act of God and not your own ...."

[The emphasis here is not in feeling 'singled out' by God to carry out 'special instructions'. Rather, it is in being so smoothly and naturally connected through your actions to the universe at large, that they no longer seem to be exclusively yours. They then belong to no single portion of the whole, only to the whole itself. Service rendered in a spirit of sacrifice constitute such connected actions.

Of course the notion that one believes one is doing 'God's will' can be rather scary, given the horrible atrocities committed with that as justification. Fortunately, Gandhi elsewhere acknowledges that all humans are fallible and that since what one person claims to be 'God's will' can be different from (even contradictory to) what another claims, then we are never justified in compelling someone else to conform to our beliefs. Our means, therefore, must be limited to non-coercive appeals to the mind and heart, and to not allowing ourselves to be seduced, coerced, or intimidated into cooperating with what we know to be wrong.]

DISCOURSE ON CHAPTER IV

The Lord says to Arjuna:

'The yoga of selfless action which I commend to you is an ancient truth; I am not propounding any new doctrine. I have declared it to you, as you are my devoted friend, in order to heal the conflict in your mind. Whenever goodness weakens and evil grows from strength to strength, I incarnate myself and protect the good and destroy the wicked. Those who are aware of this power (*maya*) of Mine are confident that evil is bound to go under. I am always by the good person's side. This person never strays from the strai[gh]t and narrow path and comes to Me at last, for such a person meditates on Me and hides in Me and thus is delivered from passion and anger and is purified by austerity and wisdom. As a person sows, so does a person reap. None can escape from the operation of the laws I have made. I established the four *varnas* (classes, not castes) by the different distribution of qualities and actions. However I am not their author, for I do not desire the fruits of action and have nothing to do with the merit or demerit arising therefrom. This divine *maya* (course of action) is worth knowing. All activities prevalent in the world are subject to divine laws, and yet God is not defiled by them. Therefore God is and also is not their author. And a person who does likewise and acts in a spirit of detachment without being defiled by actions and by the yearning for their fruit is sure to be saved. In action this person sees inaction and understands at once what is wrong action. Wrong actions are all those that are inspired by desire and cannot be performed in the absence of desire, such for instance as theft, adultery and the like. These simply cannot be done in a spirit of detachment. Therefore those who do the duty that lies nearest without desire and scheming for the fruit of the action may be said to have burnt up their actions in th[e] fire of wisdom (*jnana*). Someone who has thus abandoned the attachment to the fruit of action is always contented, always independent. Such a person has the mind under control. Such a person gives up all possessions. And this person's activity is natural like the bodily functions of a healthy individual. One can thus be free from any pride or even consciousness that one is acting on one's own. One thus has the realization that one is a mere instrument of the divine will. What then does it matter whether you meet with success or with failure? You are neither elated by the one, nor unnerved by the other. All your work is done as a sacrifice (*yajna*), that is to say, as service to the world. You will have meditated upon God in all your actions and in the end will come to God.

'There are many forms of sacrifice, the root of which lies in purity and service, such as, for instance, control of the senses, charity [chastity?] and *pranayama* (breath control) practised with a view to self-purification. Knowledge of these can be acquired from a wise teacher (*guru*) through humility, earnestness and service. If you indulge in various activities which you think are *yajna*, without any understanding of what *yajna* is, you will only do harm to yourself and to the world. It is therefore necessary that all actions should be performed intelligently. This wisdom (*jnana*) is not mere book learning. In it there is no room for doubt. It begins with faith and ends in experience. It enables one to see all beings in oneself and to see oneself in God so that everything appears to be actually informed by God. Such wisdom effects the salvation of the worst of sinners. It releases the seeker from the bondage of action, so that this seeker is not affected by its results. There is nothing else in the world so holy as this wisdom. Therefore try to obtain it with a heart full of faith in God and with the senses under control, so that you will enjoy perfect peace of mind.'

The third, the fourth and the following fifth chapter should be read together, as they explain to us what the yoga of selfless action (*anasakti*) is and what are the means of practising it. If these three chapters are properly understood, the reader will have less difficulty in tackling what follows. The remaining chapters deal in detail with the ways and means of achieving *anasakti*. We should study the Gita from this point of view, and if we pursue this study, we shall find without much trouble a solution of the problems which confront us from day to day. This calls for daily practice. Let everybody try it. If for instance one is angry, let one remember the verse dealing with anger and subdue that enemy. Supposing we heartily dislike somebody, or are impatient or gluttonous or in doubt as to whether we should do or should not do something or other, all these difficulties can be solved with the help of Mother Gita if we have faith in it and give it constant study. Our daily recitation of the Gita as well as this series of letters is a means to this end.

Supplementary Notes to Gandhi's Discourse IV

"Whenever goodness weakens and evil grows from strength to strength, I incarnate Myself and protect the good and destroy the wicked."

> [This is a very human-like portrayal of God as unfailing rescuer, which Gandhi believed literally, claiming that his life experience confirmed it time after time. I think this can also be looked upon as a way of expressing how powerful the principles and insights contained in the Gita are.
>
> Of course, this quote is the kind of statement that victims of Hitler's extermination camps might have difficulty agreeing with, and so we have introduced the age-old question, how does one reconcile the presence of terrible things in a world supposedly governed by benign forces.]

"All activities prevalent in the world are subject to divine laws, and yet God is not defiled by them. Therefore God is and also is not their author. And a person who does likewise and acts in a spirit of detachment without being defiled by actions and by the yearning for their fruit is sure to be saved."

> [Here again is the notion of conducting oneself in such a way that one is not "bound" or "defiled" by one's actions, as well as being a causal participant in events without being trapped by a self-centered attitude.
>
> This quote also seems to represent a view of "God" as the ultimate example of proper living method; as a theoretical

model of what we can attain if we try hard enough. Thus we can become 'like God'.]

DISCOURSE ON CHAPTER V

Arjuna said, 'You speak highly of wisdom, so that I am inclined to think that action is unnecessary. But then you also praise action, thus making me feel that unselfish performance of action is the thing to do. My mind will be at peace only if you tell me definitely which of the two is better.'

The Lord replied, '*Sannyasa* means wisdom and *Karmayoga* means selfless action. Both of them are good, but if I had to choose between the two, I should say that yoga or selfless action is better. The person who does not hate any one or anything, does not long for anything and is free from the pairs of opposites such as heat and cold, pleasure and pain, is a *sannyasi* (wise person, lit. one who renounces the world), no matter whether this person is or is not a performer of action. Such a person easily casts off the chain that binds. Only the ignorant speak of wisdom and action as different, not the learned. The fruit of both is the same; both lead to an identical goal. Therefore the person who sees them as one sees truly. Individuals of pure wisdom achieve their object by merely willing it, and have no need to perform an outward act. When the city of Mithila was on fire, others were bound to rush to it and fight the fire. But King Janaka contributed to this fight by his mental determination only, for his servants were ready to obey his commands. If he had run about with a water pot to quench the fire, he would only have done harm; others would have stared at him and failed to perform their own duty, or at the most would have rushed here and there with a view to the King's safety. But it is not given to every one of us to become a Janaka at once. It is indeed a very difficult task to reach a Janaka-like state. Only one in a million can reach it as the fruit of service extending over many lives, and it is not a bed of roses either. As a person goes on performing selfless action, each thought grows from strength to strength and such a person less and less resorts to external action. But such an individual is hardly conscious of this change, and this person has not this change in view either. Such a one is devoted only to service, with the result that that person's power of rendering service increases to such an extent that that individual hardly seems to rest from service. And finally such a person's service is limited to thought alone, just as an object in extraordinary motion seems to be at rest. It is obviously improper to say that such an individual does nothing. But this lofty state can, as a rule, be only imagined, and not experienced. Hence my preference for karmayoga. Millions derive the fruit of *sannyasa* (wisdom, lit. renunciation) from selfless action alone. They would fall between two stools if they tried their hand at *sannyasa*. If they take to *sannyasa*, it is very likely that they will become hypocrites, and as they have ceased to perform action, they are lost altogether. But people who have purified themselves by means of selfless action, who have their minds and senses under control and who have identified themselves with all beings, loving them as they do their own selves, — such people stand apart from action although they are acting all the time, and are not bound by it. They talk they walk, they take part in normal human activity, but their activity seems to be merely a function of their organs of sense, and they themselves seem to be doing nothing. The bodily functions of a physically healthy person are natural and spontaneous. The stomach for instance functions independently of each person, who has not to bother about its functioning. Similarly, spiritually healthy persons, though acting through their bodies, are not tainted by it and may be said to be doing nothing. Therefore one should dedicate all one's actions to Brahma (God) and perform them on Brahma's behalf, so that in spite of one's activity one does not earn either merit or demerit and is untouched by either like a lotus leaf which is untouched by water. Therefore a yogi (individual of selfless action), performing action with the body, mind and understanding in a spirit of detachment and without egotism, self-purifies and enters into peace. If one is an a-yogi, on the other hand, being attached to the fruit of action, one is then a prisoner bound by one's very own desires. The yogi lives blissfully in the city with nine gates that is the yogi's body, having renounced all actions by the mind, and realizes that in such a state the individual is not doing or getting done anything at all. The person with a purified soul does not commit sin, nor does such a person do any meritorious deed. If one acts in a spirit of detachment, having destroyed one's egotism and renounced the fruit of action, becomes a mere machine moving at the will and pleasure of the Master Mechanic or an instrument in the hands of God. The question, therefore, of such a person's earning merit or demerit does not arise. On the other hand, ignorant people are always counting their merit and demerit, and sinking deeper and deeper into the pit, so that in the end the only thing they have earned is demerit. But if one destroys one's own ignorance by wisdom from day to day, one's spontaneous actions grow purer and purer, and appear perfect and meritorious in the world's eyes. One then sees all things equal. One is equiminded towards a learned and humble Brahma (God)-knowing Brahmana, a cow, and elephant, a dog and a degraded human being who is worse than a beast. That is to say, one then serves them all with equal devotion. One does not honour any one of them or treat another with contempt. People of selfless action hold themselves to be the world's debtors, and repay what they owe to every one else and do everyone full justice. Here on earth they take the creation captive and are filled with the spirit of the Supreme. They are not elated if anybody does something pleasant; nor are they pained if foul abuse is poured upon them. Those attached to the world seek happiness from outside themselves. On the other hand those who act in a spirit of selfless detachment discover the spring of eternal peace in themselves having withdrawn the mind from external objects. All sensual pleasures are a source of pain. One should resist the rush of desire, anger and the like. The selfless yogi is constantly engaged in doing good to all creatures. The yogi's mind is free from doubt. The yogi is not of the world though being in the world. The yogi turns eyes inward by means of *pranayama* (control of breath) etc. and conquers desire, fear and anger. The yogi knows Me alone to be the supreme Lord of all, the Friend and the recipient of sacrificial offerings, and enters into My peace.'

Supplementary Notes to Gandhi's Discourse V

"free from the pairs of opposites such as heat and cold, pleasure and pain ...."

["Free from opposites" means that one is so solidly self-established that one responds appropriately and consistently no matter what the extremes of the surrounding circumstances. For example, it wouldn't matter whether or not you were comfortable, in stifling heat, or shivering in bitter cold. This would not disturb your composure. You would still be able to respond in the same way, i.e., in a way totally appropriate to the situation.]

"Only one in a million can reach it as the fruit of service extending over many lives, and it is not a bed of roses either."

[One of the virtues of the Gita is that it doesn't point to just a single set of rules; it allows of different ways of attaining an effective method for living, as appropriate to an individual's temperament and circumstances. The path of renunciation (*sannyasa*) is prohibitively difficult. Only a few will actually make it, and those only over many 'reincarnations'. But there is another way, that of **selfless action** (*karmayoga*), much easier to practice and thereby more within the reach of us all.

Even so, the road is quite difficult, and this is why the Gita is constantly exhorting us to dismiss from our lives anything that might weaken or distract us, and to focus on one goal only — union with God.

But even if we do not take the Gita literally on this, there is certainly much to be said for being disciplined, persistent, and having unity of purpose.

You will notice also that the Gita talks at length about what the 'perfect' individual is like. This is certainly admirable, but it's also important to keep in perspective one's limitations, and not to punish ourselves for falling short of the ideal, nor be discouraged from pursuing it. Anther way to look at the perfect individual is as a theoretical ideal to which we can all aim.

One very remarkable feature of Gandhi's life not much alluded to in these Discourses, is that in his striving after 'perfection' he turned everything that happened to him into a reason for working harder to improve himself. I think that much of his tenacity and success is due to the fact that, rather than be discouraged in adversity or slack off during the easy times, he would take EVERYTHING — good, bad or indifferent — and stoke it back into his blazing furnace of self-purification and self-improvement. This is certainly a valuable lesson to learn, and from a real master.]

"The stomach for instance functions independently of each person, who has not to bother about its functioning. Similarly, spiritually healthy persons, though acting through their bodies, are not tainted by it and may be said to be doing nothing. "

[This is a beautiful metaphor/explanation of what it means to act without concern for results. Our initial image of such action might include: disinterestedness, blandness, behaving 'like a sleepwalker', acting without emotion, etc. But Gandhi is telling us that, rather than this, acting without concern for results is in reality doing things totally naturally, spontaneously, unselfconsciously.]

DISCOURSE ON CHAPTER VI

The Lord said: 'One who does one's duty without any selfish desire for fruit may be called a *sannyasi* as well as a yogi. But one who abstains from action altogether is only an idler. The root of the matter is that one should not allow one's mind to flit from one object of desire to another and from that to a third. One who would practise yoga, i.e. evenness of temper (*samatvam*), cannot but perform action. Those who have achieved such evenness of temper will be serene, because their mere thoughts are charged with the strength of action. A yogi is one who is not attached to the objects of sense or to action and whose mind has ceased to roam restlessly.

'One can be saved or lost by oneself alone. Therefore you become your own friend or your own enemy as the case may be. To one who has subdued the mind, the soul is a friend; while the soul is an enemy for anyone who has failed to achieve self-control. The test for self-control is that heat and cold, pleasure and pain, honour and dishonour do not disturb one's inner serenity. One is a yogi who is a person of knowledge as well as experience, who is unwavering and master of the senses and to whom gold, stone and earth seem all alike. The yogi regards with an equal eye friend and foe, sinner and saint. With a view to attain this state you should stabilize your mind, divest it of all sensual desires, and meditate in solitude on the Supreme Soul. It is not enough to practise yogic *asanas* (postures) etc. In order to achieve evenness of temper, one must scrupulously keep the major observances (*vratas*) such as *brahmacharya* (chastity) and the like. One who thus takes one's place on a firm seat, keeps the observances and concentrates the mind on God enters into perfect peace.

'This equanimity is not for one who overeats or merely fasts, nor for one who is too much addicted to sleep or to vigils. Its seeker has to keep a sense of proportion in all action such as eating and drinking, sleeping and keeping awake. To overeat one day and fast the next day, to oversleep for a day and keep a vigil the next, to work hard for a day and pass the next in idleness is no characteristic of a yogi. The yogi is stable-minded at all times, and is without effort free from all desires. The yogi is like an unflickering lamp burning in a windless place. One is then not tossed to and fro by dramatic events on the world-stage or by one's own brain waves. Such mental poise can be acquired by slow but steady effort. The mind is fickle and restless, but it should be gradually stabilized, for one can have peace of mind only when one is firm of understanding. In order thus to stabilize the mind, you should constantly fix it on the soul. You will then see all beings in yourself and yourself in all beings, for you will see Me in all beings and all beings in Me. You who are absorbed in Me, and see Me everywhere cease to be yourself, so that you are at all times attuned to Me irrespective of what you are doing, and are incapable of sin.'

Yoga thus described seemed to Arjuna to be a tall order, and he exclaimed, 'How is one to achieve such equanimity? The human mind is restless like a monkey, and as difficult to control as the wind. How is it to be curbed?'

The Lord replied, 'You are right. But if a person earnestly sets about conquering attachment and aversion, yoga will not be difficult for that individual to practise. But it should be clear to you that it is not for one who cannot control the mind.'

Then Arjuna posed another question, 'Supposing there are those who have faith, but are lax in their effort and are thus unsuccessful in perfecting themselves, what happens to them? Are they destroyed like a broken cloud in the sky?'

The Lord said, 'Such people of faith are never lost, for no one who takes the right path ever comes to an evil end. After death they live for a time in some celestial world according to their merit and are then reborn on the earth into a holy family. But such a birth is difficult to obtain. They then regain the mental impressions developed in their former lives, and struggling harder for perfection, reach the supreme goal. Thus making an assiduous effort some attain equanimity soon, while others do so after a number of lives in accordance with the measure of their faith and endeavour. This evenness of temper is superior to asceticism, to knowledge and to sacred rites, for these latter are after all only means to the end of equanimity. Do you therefore become even-minded and a yogi. And even among yogis hold that person to be the best who dedicates everything to Me and worships Me alone in full faith.'

Pranayama (control of breath) and *asanas* (yogic postures) are referred to appreciatively in this chapter, but we should remember that at the same time the Lord has stressed the need for *brahmacharya*, i.e. keeping the observances calculated to take us nearer and nearer to God. It should be clearly understood that the mere practice of *asanas* and the like can never take us to the goal of even-mindedness. *Asanas* and *pranayama* may be of some slight help in steadying the mind and making it single-purposed, provided that they are practised to that end. Otherwise they are no better than other methods of physical training. They are very useful indeed as physical exercise and I believe that this type of exercise is good for the soul, and may be performed from a bodily standpoint. But I have observed that these practices do only harm when indulged in for the acquisition of supernormal powers (*siddhi*) and the performance of miracles. This chapter should be studied as a summary of the teaching in the preceding three chapters. It cheers us up in our spiritual struggle. We should never be downhearted and give up the endeavour to reach evenness of temper.

Supplementary Notes to Gandhi's Discourse VI

"their mere thoughts are charged with the strength of action."

> [Gandhi literally believed that, when one became sufficiently 'advanced' spiritually, thoughts translate immediately into action. He obviously felt that one is cultivating here some very powerful abilities.]

[If a seeker after perfection gets lazy and dies while in a period of regression from discipline, that person is reborn at the spot where things had been left off and may continue to advance from there.]

> [This can be taken in a less literal sense to mean that the gains one makes from leading a disciplined life are fairly persistent (like having learned to ride a bicycle). They tend to register in you at a deep level and are not so easily given up. I think also Krishna is being supportive here, telling Arjuna not to be discouraged even if he should stumble.]

"the Lord has stressed the need for *brahmacharya*, i.e. keeping the observances calculated to take us nearer and nearer to God."

> ['*Brahmacharya*' means purity of thought and action in all areas of life, including chastity as well as eating only for the purpose of sustaining life rather than for pleasure. The idea is that if you give up **seeking enjoyment**, you extricate yourself from being caught in life's sensory dead-ends, and are then left to pursue more wholeheartedly the better path.]

DISCOURSE ON CHAPTER VII

The Lord said, 'O king, I will tell you how one who devotes one's whole mind to Me, takes refuge in Me and practises karmayoga can have perfect knowledge of Me free from the shadow of a doubt. I will declare to you this knowledge based on experience, which having been known, nothing more here remains to be known. Hardly one from among thousands strives to acquire this knowledge, and perhaps one only of these strivers makes a success of it.

'Earth, water, fire, air, ether, mind, intellect and egoism — this is the eightfold composition of My *prakriti* (nature). This is the lower nature; the other is higher nature, that is, life. This world is born of these two natures, that is to say, from the coming together of body and soul. Therefore I am the cause of the origin and destruction of all things. As pearls are strung on a thread, even so is the world held together by Me. Thus I am the taste in the waters, the light in the sun and the moon, the syllable "Om" in the Vedas, the sound in ether, the spirit of enterprise in people, the sweet smell in the earth, the brightness in fire, the life in all that lives, the austerity of ascetics, the intelligence of the intelligent, the pure strength of the strong, and the craving of all beings which does not run counter to righteousness. In short you should understand that all that belongs to the states of sattva, rajas and tamas (respectively: harmony, passion, sloth; or rhythm, activity, inertia) proceeds from Me, and depends upon Me alone. People deluded by these three qualities (*gunas*) do not recognize Me Who am imperishable. My Maya made of these qualities is hard to overcome. But those who take refuge in Me pass beyond this Maya, that is, the three *gunas*. Foolish evil-doers cannot think of coming to Me even in their dreams. Being steeped in illusion, they roam in darkness and do not acquire knowledge. But the doers of good deeds worship Me. Some of them do so in order to obtain relief in their distress; others seek for knowledge of Me. A third group are inspired by a desire to get something for themselves while others worship Me with understanding, thinking it to be their duty. Worship of Me means service of My creation. This service is rendered by some because of their misery, by others in order to gain some advantage, by a third group out of curiosity as regards the outcome of such activity and by a fourth group who know what they are about and for whom service of others is something that they cannot do without. These last are My wise devotees, dearer to Me than all the rest of them. Or rather they know Me best and are nearest to Me. Their wisdom is the fruit of a quest extending over a number of lives, and when they have acquired this wisdom, they see nothing in the world except Me, Vasudeva. But those who are smitten by a variety of desires resort to other deities. I alone, however, am the giver of rewards commensurate with the devotion of each. The achievement too of these devotees of limited understanding is limited, but they rest content with it. These people in their ignorance imagine that they know Me through the senses. They do not realize that My imperishable and supreme form is beyond the reach of the senses and cannot be grasped with the hands, the ears, the nose, the eyes. Thus the ignorant do not recognize Me though I am the creator of all things. This is my *yogamaya* (creative power). Pleasure and pain are the necessary consequence of likes and dislikes and keep humankind under the influence of delusion. But those who have freed themselves from delusion and purified their thoughts and actions hold firmly to their vows and offer Me constant worship. They know Me in the form of perfect Brahma (the Absolute) as well as of individual selfs imbodied as various kinds of creatures (*adhyatma*), and My creative action (*karma*). Those who thus know Me as the One who governs the material (*adhibhuta*) and the divine (*adhidaiva*) aspects and the sacrifices (*adhiyajna*) and have attained evenness of temper are released from the bondage of birth and death after they have died. For having acquired the knowledge of reality their mind ceases to dwell on trivialities and seeing the whole universe to be filled with the spirit of God, they are absorbed in God.'

Supplementary Notes to Gandhi's Discourse VII

"[God's] imperishable and supreme form is beyond the reach of the senses and cannot be grasped with the hands, the ears, the nose, the eyes."

[What does it mean to say that God is 'beyond the senses'? I think the Gita is suggesting that we relate to the world at different levels, including in ways other than through our senses. And, further, the most **meaningful** ways to perceive and interact with reality are confused and hidden from us if we stay too close to our sensations or to the emotional urgings and reactions which they evoke. Because the whirlwind of sensory experience and desires is so overpowering, the resultant chaos unsettles our presence of mind and clouds our critical intelligence.]

DISCOURSE ON CHAPTER VIII

Arjuna asked, 'You spoke of *Brahma* (the Absolute), *adhyatma, karma, adhibhuta, adhidaiva* and *adhiyajna*, but I do not understand the meaning of all these words. Again you say that at the hour of death you are revealed to those who know you as *adhibhuta* etc. and have attained evenness of temper. Please explain all this to me.'

The Lord replied, '*Brahma* is the imperishable Supreme aspect of God, and *adhyatma* is the individual soul living in the body of all beings as the doer and the enjoyer. Karma is the process through which all beings come into existence, or in other words the process of creation. *Adhibhuta* is Myself as the perishable body, and *adhiyajna* is the individual soul purified through sacrifice. Thus whether as the body or as the foolish soul or as the purified soul or as Brahma, it is I who am everywhere. And never doubt this that one who meditates on Me in all these aspects at the hour of death, forgets oneself, is careful of nothing and desirous of nothing will be united with Me. Whatever a person constantly dwells on in the mind and remembers at the time of death is realized by that person. Therefore at all times you should remember Me and set your mind and heart upon Me and you will surely come to Me. You may say that it is hard thus to stabilize the mind. But you take it from Me that one can become single-minded by daily practice and constant endeavour, for as I told you just now, all embodied beings are in the essence Myself in various forms. For this one should prepare oneself from the very first so that one's mind does not go astray at the time for death, but is steeped in devotion, keeps the life force (*prana*) steady, and thinks only of Me as the omniscient, the ancient, the ruler, the subtle supporter of all and dispeller of ignorance like the sun which drives darkenss away.

'This supreme state is known to the Vedas as *akshara* (the Imperishable) Brahma and is reached by sages who have freed themselves from likes and dislikes. All who desire to reach it observe *brahmacharya,* i.e. keep body, mind and speech under control and give up all objects of sense in these three ways. Men and women who die, having controlled the senses and uttering the sacred syllable Om and remembering Me as they depart, reach the supreme state. Their mind is never distracted by other thoughts, and when they have thus come to Me, they are not reborn into this painful condition. To come to Me is the only means of breaking the vicious circle of birth and death.

'People measure time by the human span of a hundred years, and during that period do thousands of questionable deeds. But time is infinite. A thousand yugas (ages) make up the day of Brahma; compared with it a human day or even a hundred years of human life are as nothing. What is the use of counting such infinitesimal measures of time? Human life is as only a moment in the infinite cycle of time. It is up to us therefore to think of God alone to the exclusion of all else. How can we afford to run after momentary pleasures? Creation and dissolution have gone on unceasingly during Brahma's day and night and will do so in future too.

'Brahma who creates and dissolves beings is only an aspect of Me. Brahma is the unmanifested which cannot be perceived by the senses. Beyond this unmanifested there is yet another unmanifested aspect of Mine of which I have spoken to you. One who reaches it is not reborn, for there is not day or night so far as this is concerned. This is a calm and immovable aspect, which can be realized only by single-minded devotion. It supports and pervades the whole universe.

'It is said that one who dies in the bright half of the month during Uttarayana (the northward movement of the sun from January to July) comes to Me if that person is mindful of Me at last, and that one who dies in the dark half of the month during Dakshinayana (the southward movement from July to January) is reborn into the world. Uttarayana and the bright fortnight here may be interpreted to mean the path of selfless service; and Dakshinayana and the dark half of month mean selfishness. The path of service in the path of wisdom, and the path of selfishness is the path of ignorance. One who treads the path of wisdom is released from the bondage of birth and death while one who takes the path of ignorance becomes a bondslave. After having realized the difference between the two, who would be so foolish as to prefer to walk in the way of ignorance? All people should learn to discriminate between the paths, renounce all fruits of merit, act in a spirit of detachment and discharge their duty with all their heart and soul, and thus endeavour to reach [the] supreme state described by Me.'

Supplementary Notes to Gandhi's Discourse VIII

"Thus whether as the body or as the foolish soul or as the purified soul or as Brahma, it is I who am everywhere."

> [From this sentence and those immediately preceding, there is the at once mesmerizing and confusing notion of the oneness/manyness of God. The Gita seems to be attempting here to put into words the sense some of us have that woven throughout the fabric of life is one single powerful thread which links us with everything else through what is centralmost in us.
>
> I believe there is also here the idea that if we tend to view the world in a piecemeal, fragmented fashion, we deny ourselves a powerful technique for understanding important connections, for pulling disparate things together so as to make life more manageable and productive.]

"Whatever [someone] ... remembers at the time of death is realized by [that person]."

> [This can also be interpreted to mean that what we are at any given moment is an embodiment of what we have been and what we have devoted our time and energies to in the past. There is nothing magical about that one moment before we die. Rather, for us to be devoted at such a time means that we must have already spent a good portion of our life in disciplined practice. The Gita is not advising us simply to be ready to spring into action the

instant before death, but rather to work hard every day to improve ourselves so that we will have become as close to God as possible when critical times arrive.]

"One who treads the path of wisdom is released from the bondage of birth and death while one who takes the path of ignorance becomes a bondslave."

[This notion of attaining immortality through devotion and discipline is difficult for many of us to relate to, and seems unrealistic. But I believe it possible to interpret the 'cycle of life and death' as a metaphor for the vicious circles of life, for the self-perpetuating, self-defeating patterns that chain us to an unsatisfactory existence. The 'path of wisdom' frees us from this chain by helping us to develop stability and maturity, so that we become strong enough to avoid getting caught in those traps.

Even more comprehensively, the 'immortality' we achieve may be seen as our complete and wholehearted identification with the greater permanence of which we are a part. So, whereas our bodies may perish, we do not associate what is important in ourselves with that fact. And, whereas our senses sting with pain or sigh in pleasure, we, though totally aware of what is going on and feeling it fully, nonetheless do not become a slave to that experience.

Though death, pleasure, pain, fortune and misfortune are inescapable elements of life, our **attachment** to them is another matter altogether. By disattaching from the sensory part we can become connected in a heartfelt way to other, more important aspects.

In short, 'immortality' can be seen as being totally unneurotic about the realities of life.]

DISCOURSE ON CHAPTER IX

Having described the lofty state of a yogi in the last verse of the preceding chapter, the Lord now naturally proceeds to sing the glory of *bhakti* (devotion). For the yogi in terms of the Gita is neither a dry-as-dust person of knowledge, nor a devotee carried away by a devotee's own enthusiasm, but a selfless performer of action imbued with the spirit of wisdom as well as devotion. So the Lord said, 'As you are free from hatred, I shall now tell you the secret of wisdom, a knowledge of which will contribute to your welfare. This is the holy knowledge above all other and is easy to translate into action. Those who have no faith in it fail to find Me. People cannot perceive My unmanifested form by their senses; yet it pervades the universe. It supports the universe; the universe does not support it. Again in a sense it may be said that all these beings are not in Me, and I am not in them. Although I am the source of all beings and their sustainer, they are not in Me and I am not in them; for in ignorance they do not know Me and are not devoted to Me. Know this to be my divine mystery.

'But though it seems as if I am not in these beings, I am like the air moving everywhere. All creatures pass into My nature at the end of a cycle and are reborn at the beginning of creation. These acts are Mine, but they do not bind Me, for I act in a spirit of detachment and am indifferent as to the fruit they bear. These events happen as such is [sic.] [by?] My nature. But people do not recognize Me in such a guise and deny My existence altogether. They entertain vain aspirations, perform vain actions and are full of ignorance, so that they can be said to partake of the nature of demons. But those who abide in the divine nature know and worship Me as the imperishable creator. They are firm in their determination. They are always striving for virtue, praising Me, and meditating on Me. Others again believe Me to be one or to be many. There are countless attributes of Me; therefore those who believe Me to be many think of different attributes as so many different faces of Mine. But one and all, they are my devotees.

'I am the intention to offer a sacrifice, I the sacrifice itself, I the offering made to the spirits of the ancestors, I the herb, I the sacred verse (*mantra*), I the oblation, I the fire to which it is offered. I am the father of this world, I the mother, the supporter and the grandsire, the object of knowledge, the syllable Om, Rigveda, Samaveda and Yajurveda (the three oldest sacred books of the Hindus (*trayi*)). I am the end of the pilgrim's path, the sustainer, the lord, the witness. I am the shelter, the lover, the origin, the dissolution, heat and cold, being and non-being. Those who perform the rites mentioned in the Vedas do so in order to gain their fruit. They may thus attain the world of heaven, but they have to return to the world of mortals and to die. But if one meditates upon Me with an undistracted mind and worships Me alone, I bear all one's burdens, supply all one's needs and protect one's possessions. Some others who worship other deities with faith in their heart are victims of ignorance, but they are really worshipping Me for I am the lord of all sacrifices. However they do not know Me in My comprehensive nature and therefore are unable to reach the supreme state. Worshippers of the gods go to the world of the gods, the ancestor worshippers to the world of the ancestors and those who worship the spirits go to the spirits, while those who worship Me with the right approach come to Me. I accept the offering of love made by seekers, even if it be only a leaf or a flower. Therefore whatever you do, do it only as an offering to Me, so that your responsibility for the good and evil results will cease altogether. As you will have renounced all the fruits of action, there will be no more births and deaths for you. I am the same to all beings; none is hateful or dear to Me. But those who worship Me with devotion are in Me, and I am in them. This is not partiality but only the natural consequence of their devotion. Devotion indeed works wonders. Whoever worships Me in utter devotion becomes a saint even if that person has been a sinner. As darkness vanishes before the sun, one abandons one's evil ways as soon as one comes to Me. Therefore know for certain that My devotee shall not perish. My devotee becomes a person of religion and enters into My peace. Those who are born in the so-called lower castes and illiterates, vaishyas and shudras (the third and the fourth classes of ancient Hindu society, meaning 'farmers and merchants' and 'servants' respectively — Brahmanas (priests) and Kshatriyas (soldiers) constituted the first and the second classes. V.G.D.) who take refuge in Me come to Me. It goes without saying, that so do Brahmanas and Kshatriyas who lead a holy life. Every devotee enjoys the fruit of devotion. Therefore you who have been born in this unsubstantial world should worship Me and work out your salvation. Fix your mind on Me, be devoted to me, offer your sacrifices for My sake, prostrate yourself before Me. And if you are intent on Me reduce yourself to zero by attuning yourself to Me, you are sure to come to Me.'

Note: We learn from this chapter that devotion (*bhakti*) means attachment (*asakti*) to God. This is the royal road to the cultivation of a selfless spirit. Therefore we are told at the very beginning that devotion is the sovereign yoga and is easy to practise. It is easy to practise if it takes hold of our heart, but hard going if it does not. Hence it has been described as something for which we have to suffer our life itself as the price. But whoever has plunged into it enjoys perfect bliss though it scares the mere spectator. Sudhanva was laughing as he lay in the boiling oil while the bystanders were seized with terror and anxiety. The 'untouchable' Nanda is said to have danced as he was tried by the ordeal of fire. We need not bother whether or not these are true stories. But the fact is that a person reaches such a state of calmness and imperturbability when one is absorbed in something or other. One forgets oneself. But who would set one's heart on anything except God? 'Do not prefer the bitter nimba to sugar-cane or the glowworm to the sun and the moon'. The ninth chapter thus shows that renunciation of the fruit of action is impossible without devotion (*bhakti*). Its last verse sums up the whole chapter and in a word means, 'Seeking nothing, give yourself utterly to Me'.

Supplementary Notes to Gandhi's Discourse IX

"And if you are intent on Me and reduce yourself to zero by attuning yourself to Me, you are sure to come to Me."

[Part of what here has been called the 'sensory world' is egotism, a sense of ourselves as independent beings with a will or control over our environment. We naturally tend to relate everything that happens around us and in our bodies to our sense of self. Pain happens 'to us', pleasure 'to us', desire is 'for us', fear is a reaction to spare us pain, and so on. This kind of self-involvement promotes also a sense of self-importance, which Gandhi feels strongly we must discard if we are to live proper lives.

At first it seems like blind religious mania, or fearful lack of assertiveness, to suggest denying our 'identities', to want to 'reduce ourselves to zero'. But, the Gita says, if we think about it, we'll realize that our bodies and even our raw experiences are not 'ours' any more than they are someone else's. Any action of forces, thoughts, and materials is actually an **inter**action. Our involvement is a blend of causing and of being caused to do. Influenced by the immediacy of our raw experience, we naturally tend to overemphasize our role as agents of action, and deemphasize the rest. Thus our exaggerated sense of self is a distortion of reality, an artificial construct which we create as a reaction to raw experience, and through which everything that comes to us or goes from us is filtered.

The idea of giving up our sense of self is scary, and perhaps a bit suspect. Surrender to God, or to a teacher, is something many of us associate with religious fanaticism and cultist excesses. But the Gita does not mean for us to subordinate ourselves to others. Gandhi's struggle in India and South Africa was precisely in the opposite direction, to enable large masses of people to bring themselves out from under subordination. The Gita is instead asking us only to achieve a more realistic, balanced view of things and to live accordingly.

Somehow we are led to believe that the ego is a sign of strength. We think of it as indispensable, when in fact it's merely an artifice we use to handle the stresses of life. The idea of attempting to lose our egos seems like an abandonment of personal integrity and power, or an invitation to constant self-punishment ("I am nothing", "I am not good enough", etc.).

On the contrary, Gandhi, a good example of an 'egoless' individual, felt absolute confidence in himself, and was fully aware of his power and influence. Yet he perceived himself not as "the charismatic Mahatma Gandhi", but rather as the very ordinary Mr. Gandhi connected with the immense power of God's truth.

The ego is like an "empty fortress", apparently a stronghold, in actuality a barrier. It's not 'insufficient ego' which accounts for low self-esteem, but an unrealistically negative ego-image by which we judge against ourselves. The Gita suggests replacing all such judgments with a simple, **nonjudgmental** acceptance of reality. So, proper surrendering of our egos is not conceding worthlessness or inadequacy. It is simply rejecting that distorted view which asserts the primacy of 'me'.]

DISCOURSE ON CHAPTER X

The Lord said, 'Hear once more what I say with a view to the welfare of devotees. Even gods and great sages do not know my beginning, for the very simple reason that I am without beginning myself and am the origin of the universe including gods and sages. The wise individual who knows Me to be unborn and without beginning is liberated from all sins, for when one realizes Me as such and oneself as My child or as part and parcel of Me, one overcomes the human liability to sin. Ignorance of one's real nature is the root of sin.

'As all beings derive from Me, so do the various natures distributed to them, such as for instance forgiveness, truth, joy and sorrow, birth and death, fear and fearlessness. Those who know all these to be My glorious manifestations easily become even-minded, as they cease to be egotistic. Their heart is fixed on Me. They dedicate their all to Me. I am the only subject of their conversation. They glorify Me and live in happiness and contentment. To these loving worshippers always aware of Me I grant the power of understanding, by means of which they come to Me.'

Arjuna then praised the Lord, 'You are the supreme Brahma, the highest abode, and the Lord. You Yourself say that sages worship you as the First of the Gods, the Birthless, the All-pervading. O Lord, O Father, no one knows Your real nature; it is known to you alone. Now please tell me your glorious manifestations, and explain to me how I may recognize you by meditation.'

The Lord replied, 'There is no end to My divine manifestations, but I shall name the chief of these only. I am the *atman* (soul) dwelling in the heart of all beings. I am the beginning, the middle and the end of them all. Of the Adityas I am Vishnu. Among the lights I am the light-giving sun. Of the Maruts (wind-gods) I am Marichi. Among the stars I am the moon. Of the Vedas I am the Samveda. Of the gods I am Indra. Of the sense-organs I am the mind. Of beings I am consciousness. Of the Rudras I am Shankara (Shiva). Of the Yakshas and Rakshasas I am Kubera. Of the Daityas (demons) I am Prahlada. Of beasts I am the lion. Of birds I am the eagle. Indeed I am even the gambling of the cheats. Whatever, good or evil, happens in this world happens only by My permission. Realizing this people should give up their pride and steer clear of evil, for I am the dispenser of the fruits of their good and bad deeds. You should realize that only a single fraction of Mine sustains the entire universe.'

Supplementary Notes to Gandhi's Discourse X

"[The devotees'] heart is fixed on Me. They dedicate their all to Me. I am the only subject of their conversation."

> [This chapter talks about God being the source of everything and pervading everything. It poetically expresses the notion that we should in all ways live not for ourselves, but for God. Without attachment to ego or to the results of actions, our reference point in life then naturally becomes God, or, in other words, the universe as a whole.]

DISCOURSE ON CHAPTER XI

Arjuna, asking the Lord for a favour, said, 'O Supreme Lord, by teaching me the truth about the soul, you have dispelled my ignorance. You are All, the Creator and the destroyer, being Imperishable yourself. If possible please let me have a vision of your divine Form.'

The Lord said, 'There are thousands of my divine forms in various colours. The Adityas, the Vasus and the Rudras (various classes of Hindu gods. *Trans.*) — all are unified in My body, as well as all things, animate and inanimate. But you cannot see this my form with those fleshly eyes. Therefore I give you divine sight with which to see Me.'

Sanjaya said to Dkritarashtra, 'O king, speaking thus to Arjuna, the Lord revealed to him the Lord's marvellous form which defies description. We see a single sun in the sky every day, but supposing a thousand suns were blazing in the sky, the glory of what Arjuna saw was more dazzling then their accumulated light. The ornaments and the weapons of the Form were similarly divine. Arjuna's hair then stood erect. And he spoke, shaking all over.'

Arjuna said, 'O God, I see every thing and everybody within your body. Brahma and Shiva are there, and so are the sages and the holy serpents. I see you with countless arms and faces, and find no beginning, middle or end. You shine like a mass of insufferable light, and blaze like fire. You are the ultimate foundation of the universe, the Ancient of Days, and the guardian of eternal law. Wherever I look, I see parts of your body. The sun and the moon are your eyes as it were. You pervade heaven and earth. Your splendour burns up the universe. This world is seized with awe. The gods, the sages, and the siddhas — all are standing with clasped hands and sing your praise. On seeing their stupendous form and brilliance I lose my nerve. My patience and peace are gone O God, have mercy on [m]e. I see these people rush into your mouth frightful with tusks as moths fly into a flame and you crush them to powder. Who are you with such an awful form? I cannot understand your ways.'

The Lord said, 'I am Time, the destroyer of worlds. You may or may not fight, but the warriors on both the sides are bound to perish. You are only an instrument of the divine will.'

Arjuna said, 'O God, home of all the world, you are the Imperishable, being and non-being and what is beyond either of them. You are the First of the gods, the Ancient of Days; you are the refuge of the world. You are the one thing which is to be known. You are Vayu (wind), Yama (the God of death and judgment), Agni (fire) and Prajapati (the Creator). Hail to you a thousand times. Now please show me your original form again.'

The Lord then said, 'I showed My world-wide form to you, because I love you. You have seen today something the vision of which cannot be won by Vedic or any other studies, rituals, alms or austerities. Do not be bewildered because you have seen it. Cast away fear, be calm and see my familiar form. That shape of mine which you have seen is hard to see even for the gods and can be seen only by pure devotion. When one works for Me, one makes Me one's supreme good, becomes my devotee, frees oneself from attachment and loves all beings, comes to me.'

I have deliberately cut this as well as the last chapter short. This one is full of poetry and therefore should be read frequently either in the original or in translation, so that we may be imbued with the spirit of devotion. Whether we are or not thus imbued can be found by applying the acid test mentioned in the last verse. Devotion is impossible in the absence of total self-surrender and all-embracing love. Self-surrender and a sense of solidarity with all living beings become easy of attainment if we meditate on God as world-destroying time into whose gaping mouths the universe rushes to its doom. This fate is bound to overtake us too all of a sudden, whether we wish for it or not. Thus all distinctions of small and big, high and low, man and woman, human and the lower animals disappear. Seeing that we are all a mere morsel in the mouth of God as the Destroyer, we should become humble and reduce ourselves to zero and cultivate friendship with every one else. If we do this, we shall cease to be afraid of this terrible Form of God. On the other hand it will give us peace of mind.

Supplementary Notes to Gandhi's Discourse XI

"O God, have mercy on [m]e. I see these people rush into your mouth frightful with tusks as moths fly into a flame and you crush them to powder. Who are you with such an awful form?"

> [The God of the Gita does indeed have an 'awful form'. God here is not simply kind and generous and good, with the evil qualities relegated to Satan. Rather, God is an amalgamation of all that there is, the good together with the bad. Furthermore, God, being entirely neutral with regard to any sort of judgment of right or wrong, is beyond good and evil altogether.]

"That shape of mine which you have seen is hard to see even for the gods and can be seen only by pure devotion."

> [One gets 'closer to God' through discipline and devotion, and the closer one gets, the more clearly things are understood. As we change our lives in the proper way, life becomes less intimidating.]

DISCOURSE ON CHAPTER XII

Arjuna asks the Lord, 'Some devotees adore a personal (*sakara*) God while others worship the Absolute (*nirakara*). Which of these two courses is better?'

The Lord replies, 'Those who fix their minds on Me (as the One Life in all) with perfect faith and are absorbed in Me are My devotees indeed. But those who worship the Absolute and restrain and subdue their senses, are equiminded towards all living beings and serve them without looking on some as of a superior and others as of an inferior grade — they also will come to Me. Neither of these two classes of devotees is superior to the other. But a full realization of the Absolute is almost impossible for an embodied being. The Absolute is devoid of all attributes and thus difficult for people even to imagine. Therefore they are all worshippers of a personal God, whether they are aware of it or not.

'Do you therefore place your mind in Me (the personal God in the universal form) and offer Me your all. If this is not possible, try to restrain the aberrations of the mind; that is to say, by observing the *yamas* and *niyamas,* and with the help of *pranayama* and yogic exercies, obtain control over the mind. If even this is beyond your capacity, perform all actions for My sake, so that your delusion will be destroyed, and you will be imbued with the spirit of detachment and devotion. If you cannot do even this, renounce the fruits of action, that is, cease to have a desire for the fruits of action, and do the task which is allotted to you. One can never have any say as regards the fruit of one's action, as the nature of the fruit is determined by a number of independent factors. Be you therefore a mere instrument in My hands. I have thus described four methods, none of which is superior to the others. You may adopt any one of the four you like. It may seem as if the path of knowledge (hearing the doctrine, pondering over it, etc.) is easier to take than that of *yamas, niyamas, pranayama, asanas,* etc., meditation in worship is easier still and the renunciation of the fruit the easiest of all. But the same method is not equally well suited for all. And some seekers have to adopt all the four methods, which are inter-connected. You must become a devotee one way or other; you may take any path that leads to this destination.

'Let me tell you what the true devotes are like. They do not hate or bear ill-will to any living creature. They look on all with love and compassion. They are free from the delusion of "I" and "Mine". They reduce themselves to zero. Pleasure and pain are equally acceptable to them. They forgive the wrong-doer even as they expect to be forgiven themselves. They are always contented with their lot, and are unshakable in their resolve. They dedicate their intellect and mind and all to Me. They never molest their fellow-creatures; these are therefore never afraid of them. They do not allow themselves to become perturbed by the world. They are free from exultation, sorrow, anger, fear and the like. They seek nothing for themselves. They are pure and skilful in action. They renounce every undertaking. Although they are firm in their resolve, they are indifferent as regards the success or failure of their action; that is to say, they are not anxious about its result. They are alike to friend and foe. Honour and insult are the same to them. They are silent and content with what comes. They move freely as if they were alone. They have a steady mind at all times and places. A devotee who behaves like this in faith is dear to me.'

Q. The devotee 'renounces all undertakings.' What does this mean?

A. The devotee will not draw up schemes of future expansion. For example, if a merchant who deals in cloth now has any plans of selling firewood as well in the future, or if this merchant, having one shop only, thinks of opening five more shops, that would be *arambha* (undertaking) on the merchant's part, and the devotee will have none of it. This principle is applicable to service of the nation as well. For instance a worker in the Khadi department today will not take up cow-keeping tomorrow, agriculture the day after and medical aid on the fourth day. One will do one's best in whatever has come to one. When I am free from egoism, nothing remains for me to do.

'The Lord has bound me with a cotton thread; I am the Lord's, no matter where the Lord leads me. I have been stabbed with the dagger of love.' A devotee's every activity is planned by God. It comes to the devotee as in the natural course of things. The devotee therefore rests content with, 'this, that or anything else'. This is the meaning of 'renouncing all undertakings.' The devotee does not cease to work; indeed such a person is nothing if not a worker. The devotee only ceases to think needless thoughts about work accomplished. It is these that he has to renounce.

'This has been acquired by me today; that purpose I shall gain tomorrow' — this is the opposite of 'renouncing undertakings.'

Supplementary Notes to Gandhi's Discourse XII

"The Absolute is devoid of all attributes and thus difficult for people even to imagine. Therefore they are all worshippers of a personal God, whether they are aware of it or not."

> [Because of our particular human physical form ('embodiment'), and our social/cultural context, we are limited in our ability to observe, perceive and analyze. God, as the extremely complex phenomenon underlying all things, cannot therefore be totally understandable to us and we are thereby incapable of forming an accurate image of God. Since our connections to things must be in ways we can grasp and relate to, we tend to see God as personal and human-like.
>
> Of course, acknowledgement of our limits to understand need not (indeed, it **should** not) prevent us from acting as best we can **within** these limits, going by whatever information is available, and using whatever abilities we possess.
>
> However, it is not the particular image or personality that we ascribe to things in general — to God, if you will — that is important. It is our active, heartfelt connection to God, and how we

can sustain, nurture and build upon that connection.

Acknowledging his imperfection, Gandhi was non-condescendingly able to validate characterizations of God different from his own. He saw the images of God as represented in various different religions (together with their diverse rituals, rites and so forth) all as crutches to help many different kinds of people with a variety of cultural backgrounds keep on the path of selflessness and devotion. Thus, while devoutly following Hinduism, he was able to respect other religions, not putting his above them.

Nor did Gandhi seek to impose Hinduism on anyone else. Instead, he encouraged people to become better practitioners of their own religions. This is a very healthy attitude, which it would be nice to see more of in the world.]

"renounce all undertakings. ... if [a] merchant ... thinks of opening up ... more shops, that would be ... undertaking ...."

[It might seem to be suggested here that a person who wants to be close to God shouldn't make any plans for the future. But I believe what the Gita is really saying is that one should not make plans for self-aggrandizement, or to plan in such a way that one is drawn away from the selfless uncomplaining acceptance of whatever comes one's way.

But it also should be realized that, so far as Gandhi believed, **any** planning for the future in order to stave off possible unpleasant consequences indicates a lack of faith in God.]

DISCOURSE ON CHAPTER XIII

The Lord said, 'Kshetra (the Field) is another name for the human body and kshetrajna means one who knows the Field. Understand Me as the knower of the Field in all bodies. Real knowledge means discrimination between the Field and the knower of the Field. The five great elements, namely, earth, water, fire, air and ether, individually (*ahamkara*), intellect, the unmanifest, the ten senses (the five organs of perception, viz. hearing, touch, sight, taste and smell, and the five organs of action, viz., tongue, feet, hands and the organs of evacuation and reproduction) mind, the five sense objects, desire and hatred, pleasure and pain, *sanghata* (the power of combination inherent in the constituents of the body), consciousness and cohesion, — these constitute the Field with its modifications. Knowledge of these is essential, as they have to be renounced. Wisdom is the foundation on which such renunciation can be based. Wisdom here means and includes humility, unpretentiousness, non-violence, forgiveness, rectitude, service of the teacher, purity, steadfastness, self-restraint, indifference to sense objects, absence of egoism, insight into the evil of birth, death, old age, disease and pain, detachment from spouse and children, hearth and home, friends and relations, equimindedness to good and bad fortune, wholehearted devotion to God, love of solitude, dislike for the enjoyment of sensual pleasures in company with others, thirst for knowledge of the soul, and at last the beatific vision. And the reverse of this is ignorance. Now let me tell you something about that which has to be known with a view to salvation. That is beginningless supreme Brahma. Brahma is beginningless because it is unborn and was there when there was nothing. It is neither *sat* (existent) nor *asat* (non-existent) but beyond them both. But from another standpoint it can be called *sat*, because it is eternal. Human beings cannot recognize it as such; therefore it is said to be beyond even *sat*. It pervades the whole universe. It may be said to have a thousand hands and feet, and though it seems to have hands and feet, it is devoid of the organs of sense or it does not need these organs. Sense organs are transitory while Brahma is eternal. And although being all-pervasive and all-sustaining, it may be said to be enjoying the qualities (*gunas*), it is free from them. Where there are *gunas*, there is change (*vikara*), but Brahma is changeless. It may be said to be outside all beings, because it is out for those who do not know it. And it is within all beings as it is all-pervading. Similarly it is both moving and unmoving. It is subtle and hence imperceptible. It is distant as well as near. It is undivided in the sense that it is imperishable though name (*nama*) and form (*rupa*) perish, but it also seems to be divided as we say that it is within all creatures. It creates, preserves and destroys. It is the light of lights beyond darkness, and the end of all knowledge. Brahma which is planted in every heart is *jneya*, the one thing worth knowing. All knowledge is a means to the end of being united with it.

'God and God's *maya* (nature) are both without beginning. Modifications (*vikaras*) are born of *maya* and these give rise to various kinds of action (*karma*). On account of *maya*, the soul experiences pleasure and pain and the fruit of merit (*punya*) and demerit (*papa*). One who, having realized this, does one's duty in a spirit of detachment is not born again in spite of his activity, for one beholds the face of God in all faces, and seeing that not a leaf moves but by the divine will, one is free from egotism, understands that one is separate from the body and that the soul, though living in the body, remains by means of knowledge unaffected like the omnipresent ether.'

Supplementary Notes on Gandhi's Discourse XIII

"Wisdom here means and includes humility, unpretentiousness, non-violence ... detachment from spouse and children, hearth and home, friends and relations ...."

> [What has been translated as 'wisdom', doesn't just mean intellectual understanding, or even understanding at the 'gut level', but rather understanding combined with **living** in the proper way. A 'wise' person is therefore not simply one who knows a great deal about the correct principles of life, but one who actually lives according to those principles.

As before, "detachment" does not mean lack of feeling, disinterestedness, or lack of caring; it means not being hooked in — even to those you hold most dear. The Gita encourages us to relate to people and things through our relationship with God, which must remain foremost. Detachment and equimindedness are both promoters and indicators of the depth of that relationship.]

DISCOURSE ON CHAPTER XIV

The Lord said, 'Once more I will teach you that supreme wisdom which enabled sages to reach the highest perfection. People who find that wisdom and do their duty accordingly are delivered from the cycle of births and deaths. O Arjuna, know me to be the father and mother of all beings. The three *gunas* born of nature, viz. *sattva* (goodness), *rajas* (passion), and *tamas* (ignorance) bind the soul down. They may be described respectively as the highest, the middling and the lowest. Of these *sattva* is pure and unsullied and gives light; it is therefore the source of happiness. *Rajas* arises from attachment and craving and makes a person indulge in all manner of activities. *Tamas* is rooted in ignorance and delusion and makes one negligent and indolent. In short *sattva* makes for happiness, *rajas* for restlessness and *tamas* for sloth. Sometimes *sattva* prevails, overpowering *rajas* and *tamas*; at other times *rajas* prevails, overpowering *sattva* and *tamas*; at still other times *tamas* prevails, overpowering *sattva* and *rajas*. When the light of wisdom shines through all the activities of the body it may be known that *sattva* is increasing. Where greed, bustle, unrest and competition are observed, *rajas* is the ruler. And the predominance of *tamas* is characterized by ignorance, sloth and delusion. If *sattva* prevails in one's life, one is born in the sinless worlds of the great sages after death. If *rajas* dominates one's life, one is born among those who are attached to action. And if *tamas* is the ruling principle, one returns to the womb of the senseless. The fruit of *sattvika* action is purity, while the fruit of *rajas* is pain and the fruit of *tamas* is ignorance. A *sattvika* person rises to the higher regions; a *rajasa* person remains in this world, while a *tamasa* individual sinks to the underworld. When someone perceives no doer of action other than these qualities and knows Me who am beyond them this person enters into My nature. When the dweller in the body has overcome the three qualities from which all bodies arise, that person is freed from birth and death, old age and pain and drinks the nectar or eternal life.'

On hearing that who transcends the qualities makes such great progress on the pilgrim's path, Arjuna asked,

'What are the marks of such perfection? If one is a perfect being, how does one conduct oneself? And how does such a person cross over the qualities?'

The Lord replied, 'You are said to have risen above the qualities when you are not angry if the light and knowledge of *sattva* or the activity and bustle of *rajas* or the delusion and ignorance of *tamas* are there and are not wishful if they are not. You sit like one who is unconcerned and is not disturbed by the qualities. You stand apart unmoved, being aware that they are the doers of all actions. You are even-minded to pleasure and pain as well as to a lump of earth, a stone and gold. The pleasant and the unpleasant are alike to you. You are unaffected by either praise or blame. You are the same in honour and evil fame. You are alike to friend and foe. And you have abandoned all undertakings.

'Do not think that this is a goal you can never reach and that therefore you need not exert yourself. What I have described is the state of a perfect individual. The way to it is to serve Me with single-minded devotion. From the third chapter onwards I have pointed out that a human being cannot so much as even breathe without action (*karma*), from which no one can ever hope to escape. If you would transcend the qualities you should dedicate all your actions to Me, and cease to desire their fruits. If you do this, your actions will not be an impediment to your progress, for I am Brahma, immortal life, the eternal law and joy for ever.

'When you reduce yourself to zero, you see Me alone everywhere. You are *guna-atita* (one who has crossed over the qualities).'

Supplementary Notes to Gandhi's Discourse XIV

"[The perfect individual sits] like one who is unconcerned and is not disturbed by the qualities."

> [The 'perfect' individual (which is to say, the ideal to which we should aspire), may seem, as characterized here, to be blasé and constricted. Such a person is portrayed as continually exercising restraint so as not to be moved by desires or sensations. Is the Gita here encouraging us

to deaden our emotions, to stifle spontaneity? This, though an easy trap to fall into along the way, is nonetheless not what the Gita is recommending. And it certainly is not characteristic of Gandhi.

He bubbled with lively humor and, though careful and meticulous, remained relaxed and spontaneous. Gandhi was, furthermore, deeply impassioned in everything he did, being at the same time quite unconcerned about (disattached from) future results.

Restraint combined with emotional charge and spontaneity is, admittedly, a difficult combination to achieve, and I'm not so sure the Gita is as thorough as it could be in showing us how to achieve it. But in the ideal condition an individual experiences emotion and bodily sensations as intensely as anyone, yet has weeded out tension, hostility, inner conflict, worry, and drivenness either towards pleasure or away from pain. In short, while 'enjoying' the senses (experiencing them fully), an 'advanced' person is not 'bound' by (caught up in) them. And the more advanced one gets, the less vigilance and conscious effort of restraint is required.

Also, on the opposite side of this coin, as we mature and develop, as we become more and more released from anxieties and conflicts, we experience a progressively more relaxed, vivid, **positive** connection to people and life in general.]

DISCOURSE ON CHAPTER XV

The Lord said, 'This world is like an *ashvattha* (sacred fig) tree with roots above and branches below and with the Vedic hymns as its leaves. And whoever knows it knows the Vedas. The branches of this cosmic tree nourished by the qualities 'shoot to heaven and sink to earth' (Sir Edwin Arnold). Sense objects are its sprouts. It is these things of the senses which bind the soul with the bonds of *karma* in the world of people.

'The real nature of this tree cannot be known here, nor its beginning, nor end, nor foundation.

'This strongly rooted cosmic tree should be cut down with the weapon of non-co-operation, so that the soul may rise to a higher world from which there is no return to the world of mortals. With this end in view you should engage yourself in the constant worship of the Ancient of Days, from whom all this activity (the cosmic process) seems to flow. The wise person who is free from pride and delusion, victorious over the vice of attachment and devoted to the Supreme Soul, who is free from cravings and to whom pleasure and pain are alike, — that wise person reaches the state which is beyond all change, and which does not need to be illumined by the sun, the moon or fire. That is My supreme abode.

'An eternal part of Myself transformed into the individual soul in this world draws to itself the senses including the mind which reside in matter. When the soul enters the body or leaves it, it takes these senses with it even as the wind carries fragrance from its places. It enjoys sense objects with the help of the ear, the eye, the senses of touch and taste, the nose and the mind. The ignorant cannot recognize it as it goes or stays or enjoys itself under the influence of the qualities, but the sages see it with the eye of wisdom. Striving *yogis* see it living in their own bodies, but those who have not achieved evenness of temper cannot see it even if they try.

'The light of the sun that illumines all the world, that which is in the moon and in fire, — know that all that light is Mine. Permeating the soil I sustain all living beings. I become the sap-producing moon and feed the plants. Becoming the fire of life in the bodies of all living creatures and being united with the life breaths, I digest four kinds of food. I abide in all hearts. From Me are memory and wisdom as well as their absence. I am that which is to be known by all the Vedas. So also I am the author of Vedanta and the knower of the Vedas.

'There may be said to be two kinds of personalities in this world, namely *kshara* (the perishable) and *a-keshara* (the imperishable). The perishable is all beings; and the imperishable is I who inspire them, and am the same for ever. But beyond either is the highest spirit who is called the Supreme Soul, and who, pervading all, sustains the three worlds. This too is I. I therefore transcend the perishable and even the imperishable, and am known in the world as well as in the Vedas as the supreme reality. The wise people who recognize Me as such know all that need be known, and serve Me with their whole being.

'O sinless Arjuna, I have told you this most secret teaching. By knowing this a person becomes truly wise and reaches the shores of salvation.'

DISCOURSE ON CHAPTER XVI

The Lord said, 'I will now point out the distinction between the divine and the demoniacal natures. Among the signs of the divine are fearlessness, purity of heart, wisdom, evenness of temper, self-control, alms-giving, sacrifice, study of the scriptures, austerity, straightforwardness, non-violence, truth, freedom from anger, renunciation, peacefulness, not speaking evil of others, compassion to all living beings, absence of greed, gentleness, modesty, absence of fickleness, vigour, forgiveness, fortitude, purity, internal as well as external, freedom from malice and pride.

'Among the signs of the demoniacal are hypocrisy, arrogance, conceit, anger, cruelty and ignorance.

'The divine nature leads to liberation while the demoniacal leads to bondage. Arjuna, you are born with the endowments of the divine nature.

'I will say something more about the demoniacal nature, so that people may easily give it up. Persons of such a nature do not know what to do and what to refrain from doing. There is no purity or truth in them, so that they do not observe the rules of good conduct.

'They hold that the world is unreal, without basis or ruler. For them sex is all the world so that they think of nothing except enjoyment of the objects of sense.

'They do horrible deeds. They are dull-witted. They hold fast to their wicked thoughts and all their activity is directed only to the destruction of the world. Their desires are insatiable. They are full of hypocrisy, pride and arrogance. They are thus plagued by innumerable cares. They want fresh sensual pleasures every day. They are "ensnared

In nooses of a hundred idle hopes" (Arnold),

and by unlawful means amass wealth in order to gratify their desires.

'"I got this today; I will get that tomorrow. I killed this one enemy today; I will also kill others. I am a person of might. I have great possessions. Who is my equal? With a view to fame I will sacrifice to the gods, give alms and make merry". They say this to themselves with a chuckle, and being caught in the net of delusion, go to hell at last.

'People with such a nature, given over to pride, speak ill of others and thus hate God who dwells in all hearts. They are therefore frequently born in the wombs of degraded parents.

'There are three gates to hell, leading to the ruin of the soul: lust, anger and greed. Therefore we should renounce them all. Turning aside from them, people go by the strai[gh]t and narrow path and reach the highest state.

'One who disregards the scriptures composed of eternal principles and gives oneself up to pleasure cannot attain happiness or peace characteristic of the right way.

'Therefore in deciding what you must do and what you must not do, you should acquire the knowledge of fundamental and immutable principles from wise people and think and act accordingly.'

Supplementary Notes to Gandhi's Discourse XVI

"the divine and the demoniacal natures."

> [The divine vs. demonic here is not really hero vs. villain, but rather a metaphor for the best in us, according to which we live gratifyingly and successfully, and the worst in us, with which we make our own (and others') hell. The horrible suffering that people manage to inflict on themselves and others comes, according to the Gita, from selfishness, laziness, and yielding to urges. If you've gotten past your ego and feel a part of yourself in others as well as others in yourself, you cannot bring yourself to harm anything, because from that perspective it's only hurting yourself.]

"One who ... gives oneself up to pleasure ... cannot attain happiness or peace characteristic of the right way."

> [This is perhaps the most difficult part of the Gita (and of much of Eastern

religion in general) to comprehend. Certainly our intuition tells us that pleasure feels good and pain bad. How can both be equal, and both be wrong? And again, there is no tight logical argument here, only an appeal to the experience of those who give evidence of having gotten beyond the sensory pleasures entirely.]

DISCOURSE ON CHAPTER XVII

Arjuna asked, 'What happens to those who serve in faith, neglecting the prevailing code of conduct?'

The Lord replied, 'There are three kinds of faith, characterized by *sattva, rajas* and *tamas* as the case may be. As is a person's faith, so is that individual.

'*Sattvika* people worship the gods; *rajasa* people worship demigods and demons; and *tamasa* people worship the spirits of the dead.

'The nature of a person's faith cannot be ascertained offhand. In order to assess it correctly one must know the precise nature of that person's food, austerity, sacrifice and alms-giving.

'Foods which make for long life and increase the vital force, energy, strength and health are said to be *sattvika*. *Rajasa* foods are violently bitter, sour, hot or pungent and give rise to disease and aches and pains. And cooked food which is stale or gives out a bad smell and the leavings of others are said to be *tamasa*.

'The sacrifice which is offered as a matter of duty without expecting a reward and with mental concentration is said to be *sattvika*. A *rajasa* sacrifice is that in which a reward is desired and which is offered for outward show. And a *tamasa* sacrifice is one in which scriptural rules are disobeyed, no eatables or alms are given away and no hymns are chanted.

'Honouring the saintly, purity, *brahmacharya* and non-violence constitute austerity of the body. Truthful, pleasant and beneficial speech as well as a study of the scriptures is austerity of the speech. And cheerfulness, gentleness, silence, self-control and purity of motive — these are called the austerity of the mind. Such austerity of the mind, body and speech as is practised without desire of fruit by people with an evenness of temper is said to be *sattvika*. Austerity practised for ostentation and with a view to gaining honour is said to be *rajasa*. And the gift which is given in a contemptuous spirit, and without honour done to the recipient and without considering the proper time and place for it is said to be *tamasa*.

'Brahma is designated in the Vedas as *Om tat sat*. Therefore people of faith pronounce the sacred syllable

OM when they commence any rite of sacrifice, almsgiving or austerity. This single syllable stands for Brahma. *Tat* means **that.** And *sat* means *satya*, beneficent. That is to say, God is one, God alone is, God alone is truth and the benefactor of the world. A person who offers a sacrifice, makes gifts or practises austerity with a realization of this truth and in a spirit of dedication is someone of *sattvika* faith. And one is free from blame if one knowingly or unknowingly does something different from the correct procedure in the spirit of dedication. But acts undertaken in the absence of such a spirit are said to be performed without faith and therefore are *asat* (unreal).'

DISCOURSE ON CHAPTER XVIII

Even after he had pondered over the teaching in all the previous chapters, there was still a doubt in Arjuna's mind. So he said, 'The *sannyasa* of the Gita seems to be different from renunciation as currently understood. Are *sannyasa* and *tyaga* really different?'

While resolving Arjuna's doubt in answer to this question, the Lord summarized the Gita doctrine in a concise manner: 'Some actions are motivated by desire. Various activities are indulged in by people with a view to fulfil[l] various desires. These are called *kamya* actions. Then again there are certain necessary and natural actions such as breathing, eating, drinking, lying down, sitting etc. with a view to keep the body a fit instrument of service. And thirdly there are actions done with a view to serve others. Giving up *kamya* actions is *sannyasa*, and renunciation of fruits of all actions is tyaga as recommended to you all along.

'Some people maintain that there is evil, no matter how little, in all actions whatever. Even so, a person must not give up actions done with a view to *yajna* (sacrifice), that is to say, the service of others. Almsgiving and austerity are included in *yajna*. But even while serving others, a person should act in a spirit of detachment. Otherwise this person's activity is likely to be mixed up with evil.

'Renunciation owing to ignorance of duties that must be done is said to be inspired by *tamas*. Giving up any action merely because it involves physical suffering is said to be *rajasa*. But service rendered to others because of a feeling that it must be done and without the desire for the fruits is real *sattvika tyaga*. In this *tyaga* therefore there is no giving up of all actions, but only of the fruit of duties that must be done, and of course of other, that is, *kamya* actions. When wise individuals act in such a selfless spirit, all their doubts are dispelled, their motives are pure and they have no thought of personal comfort and discomfort.

'One who does not abandon the fruits of action must enjoy or put up with the natural consequences of one's own acts, and is thus a bond-slave for ever. But one who gives up the fruits of action achieves freedom.

'And why should people feel attachment for action? It is idle for people to imagine that they themselves are the doers. There are five causes for the accomplishment of all actions, namely, this body, the doer, the various instruments, efforts, and last but by no means the least, providence.

'Realizing this, you should give up pride. If you do something without egoism you may be said to be not doing it in spite of your doing it, for you are not bound by your action. Of humble people who have reduced themselves to zero it may be said that you do not kill though you kill. This does not mean that such people in site of their humility may kill and yet be unaffected by the killing. For no occasion can arise for such people to indulge in violence.

'There are three things that inspire action: knowledge, the object of knowledge and the knower. And there are three constituents of action: the organ, the deed and the doer. The thing to be done is the object of knowledge; the method of doing it is knowledge and one who knows it is the knower. After one has thus received an impulse to action, one performs an action in which the senses serve as instruments. Thought is thus translated into action.

> 'That by which a [person] is able
> To see one changeless Life in all the
> lives'
>
> (Edwin Arnold)

and to realize the essential unity that underlies all diversities is *sattvika* knowledge. In *rajasa* knowledge one holds that there are different souls in different creatures, while in *tamasa* knowledge a person does not know a thing and imagines that everything is mixed up without rhyme and reason.

'Similarly there are three kinds of action. Action in which there are no likes and dislikes and no desire for personal gains is *sattvika*. That in which there is a desire for enjoyment, egoism and restlessness is *rajasa* action. And *tamasa* action is one in which no thought at all is given to personal capacity and consequential injury or violence and which is undertaken through delusion.

'So also there are three classes of doers. A *sattvika* doer is free from attachment and egoism and yet firm and enterprising and is neither elated by success nor worried by failure. A *rajasa* doer is impassioned, greedy and violent, "slave by turns of sorrow and of joy" (Edwin Arnold) and of course desires to obtain the fruit of actions performed. And a *tamasa* doer is unsystematic, procrastinating, obstinate, malicious and indolent; in short, without an iota of self-culture.

'Intellect, firmness and happiness also are said to be of three kinds. The *sattvika* intellect is able properly to distinguish between action and non-action,

> "What must be done, and what must
> not be done,
> What should be feared, and what
> should not be feared,
> What binds and what emancipates
> the soul."
> (Edwin Arnold)

The *rajasa* intellect tries to draw these distinctions but generally fails to do so correctly, while the *tamasa* intellect "looks upon wrong as right and sees all things contrariwise of truth" (Edwin Arnold).

'Firmness is the power of taking up some thing and sticking to it through thick and thin. It is more or less inherent in all things; otherwise the world could not subsist for a single moment. Firmness is *sattvika* when there is a constantly maintained balance between the activities of the mind, the vital airs (*pranas*) and the senses. The firmness by which one holds fast to duty, pleasure and wealth from attachment and with a view to personal advantage is *rajasa*. And firmness is *tamasa*, "wherewith the fool

> Cleaves to ... sloth, ... sorrow and
> ... fears ... vanity and despair."
> (Edwin Arnold)

'*Sattvika* happiness is the
"pleasure that endures,
Banishing pain for aye, bitter at
first

As poison to the soul, but
afterwards
Sweet as the taste of Amrit."
(Edwin Arnold)
It arises from true self-
knowledge.
'*Rajasa* happiness arises
from sensual enjoyment.
". . . Sweet
As Amrit is its first taste,
but its last
Bitter as poison."
'And *tamasa* happiness is
that
". . . which springs
From sloth and sleep and
foolishness."
(Edwin Arnold)

'This threefold classification is thus applicable to all things. The duties of the four *varnas* (classes in ancient Hindu society) are fixed by reason of the dominance or recession of the qualities planted in each.

'A Brahmana's conduct is characterized by calmness, self-discipline, austerity, purity, forgiveness, uprightness, wisdom, experience and faith in God. The characteristics of a Kshatriya are valour, splendour, firmness, resourcefulness, not flying from battle, open-handedness and leadership. A Vaishya's task is "to till the ground, tend cattle, venture trade" (Edwin Arnold), and service is the Shudra's work. This is not to say that a member of any one of these classes may not be endowed with qualities characteristic of other classes or is not entitled to cultivate them in himself. But qualities and work as mentioned above serve as signs for the recognition of a person's *varna*. If the qualities and tasks of each caste are recognized, there is no undesirable competition or feeling of hatred among them. There is no question here of high and low. But if we each do our duty selflessly according to our nature, we will reach perfection. Therefore one's own duty, though it appears to be valueless, is better than the duty of another which seems to be easy. You may remain free from sin when you perform the task naturally allotted to you, as you are then free from selfish desires; the very wish to do something else arises from selfishness. For the rest, all actions are clouded by defects as fire by smoke. But the natural duty is done without desire for its fruit, and thus loses its binding force.

'Those calm yogis who have been sanctified by thus performing their own duty, who have the mind under control, who have given up the five sense objects, who have overcome likes and dislikes, who live in solitude, i.e. whose eyes are turned inward, who achieve mastery of the mind, body and speech by abstemiousness, who are ever conscious of the living presence of God and are absorbed in Him. Thus taking refuge in Me, they gain the eternal place.

'Therefore dedicate your all to Me, regard Me as the supreme object of your love, and with discrimination, fix your mind on Me. As you do this, you will overcome all difficulties. But if out of egotism you do not listen to Me, you will perish. The one thing needful is that abandoning all conflicting views, you should come to Me alone for shelter, and thus be freed from sin.

'Do not tell this truth to anyone who is not a devotee, austere in life, and hating Me, does not wish to listen. But one who communicates this great secret to My devotees will surely come to me in virtue of devotion.'

After having thus reported to Dhritarashtra the dialogue between Arjuna and Krishna, Sanjaya said,

'Where there is Krishna, the prince of yoga, and Arjuna with his bow and arrows, there are prosperity, victory, happiness and fundamental morality.'

Krishna to whom the epithet 'prince of yoga' has here been applied means pure knowledge based on spiritual experience, and by referring to Arjuna as an archer it is suggested that where there is action in accordance with such knowledge, the doer obtains every wish that is not contrary to lofty morals.

Supplementary Notes to Gandhi's Discourses XVII and XVIII

[These chapters discuss the austerities, sacrifices, renunciation, alms-giving, and other rites which, according to the Hindu religious scriptures, one must practice in order to achieve closeness to God.

Those scriptures tend to place people and their actions into three basic categories, *sattva, rajas*, and *tamas*, referring (roughly) to knowledge/understanding, emotionality/desires, and fear/laziness, respectively, as discussed in this and previous chapters. But the emphasis here should not be on those specific acts recommended, or the sorts of categories in which the Hindu religion places them, but rather on the spirit in which all actions in one's life are performed. You are encouraged to focus here not on what is peculiar to the Hindu religion, but rather on an overall perspective of the Gita's message, seeking to understand what you, whether or not you happen to be Hindu, can benefit by.]

TRANSLATOR'S NOTES

Chapter I

'I regard Duryodhana and his party as the baser impulses in people, and Arjuna and his party as the higher impulses. The field of battle is our own body. An eternal battle is going on between the two camps. ... Krishna is the Dweller within, ever whispering in a pure heart. Like the watch the heart needs the winding of purity; or else the Dweller ceases to speak' (M. K. Gandhi: **Hindu Dharma**, Navajivan, 1950, p. 156).

Chapter II

'English friends made me read the Gita.... They placed before me Sir Edwin Arnold's magnificent rendering of the Gita. I devoured the contents from cover to cover and was entranced by it. The last ninteen verses of the second chapter have since been inscribed in the tablet of my heart. They contain for me all knowledge. The truths they preach are the "eternal verities."...

'Those verses are the key to the interpretation of the Gita' (ibid., p. 152).

'The message of the Gita is to be found in the second chapter where Krishna speaks of the balanced state of mind, of mental equipoise. In nineteen verses at the close he explains how this state can be achieved. It can be achieved, he tells us, after killing all your passions. It is not possible to kill your brother after having killed all your passions' (ibid., p. 179).

'I have endeavoured to show that its message consists in the performance of one's duty with detachment. The theme of the Gita is contained in the second chapter and the way to carry out the message is to be found in the third chapter. This is not to say that the other chapters have less merit. Indeed every one of them has a merit of its own.

'I hope that those who take part in the ... celebration [of *Gitajayanti*] will approach it in the proper spirit and with a fixed intention to live up to the message of the noble song' (ibid., p. 182).

A fittingly anonymous article in **The Times** of November 17, 1956 will serve as a fine commentary on the Gita doctrine:

'In the collect for tomorrow (the twenty-fifth Sunday after Trinity) prayer is offered that those who "bring forth the fruit of good works" may be "rewarded by God." There seems to be a conflict between morality and religion at this point. For while the former is emphatic that good actions must be done without the thought of reward and makes its motto "duty for duty's sake", the latter insists that God makes a distinction between good and evil, so that one meets with God's approval while the other is condemned, and uses to express this the common language of reward and punishment.

'Did not Jesus himself say, "What shall it profit [one to] gain the whole world and lose [one's] own soul?" Yet his life is clear evidence that the only service of God he valued was one that is free from any taint of self-interest. His fidelity was unshaken even when it became clear that it would lead him to abandonment by his friends and death at the hands of his enemies. The cross is a reminder that devotion to God and love to people, if they are rewarded at all, must find their reward elsewhere than in popular approval or material advantage.

'What then are the rewards of which the collect speaks? The answer is to be found in the words: "Blessed are the pure in heart, for they shall see God." The reward of service is not something attached to the service to make it worthwhile; it is of the same order as the service itself. Inner dedication to God leads to admission into God's fellowship and deeper knowledge of God's will: the love of God makes possible an ever closer likeness to God. The vision of God, the enrichment of one's whole being, the joy of co-operation with God in the enterprises of God's kingdom — these are the rewards that God bestows on God's servants.

'Yet that is not all. While it is true that the primary rewards to the life of the spirit are in the realm of the spirit, it is also true that character and uprightness may bring substantial advantages at a lower level. There have been cases in which public opinion has rallied to a leader just because this leader was known to be entirely honest and disinterested, giving this individual power and office that it would not entrust to a meaner person. To be scrupulously fair and absolutely reliable in business may bring advantages that do not fall to the lot of those who think only in terms of immediate profits.

'Not, of course, that action is to be for such gains. The maxim that "honesty is the best policy" is a dangerous one. Whoever chooses honesty for the returns it yields may be tempted to abandon it when circumstances arise in which it looks likely to be unprofitable. The paradox is that a virtue such as honesty leads to esteem and success when it is practised for its own sake, without any thought either of esteem or of success. Religion and morality are alike injured by any appeal to self-interest; the reward God gives is the vision of God, and this is for those only who serve God without thought of what will be lost and what will be gained thereby.

'Perhaps this paradox that the rewards of God's service are for those only who serve God with no thought of reward lies behind the saying of Jesus that whoever would save one's life will lose it while whoever is prepared to lose it will find that life has in fact been preserved. God receives into the choicest company of God's servants those who follow truth and right simply because they are truth and right, and do not ask what the outcome of their fidelity will be. In the great words of Ignatius Loyola, they labour and do not ask for any reward save that of knowing that they do God's will.'

Chapter XII

[']Whenever I meet any one who knows the Gita by heart, he or she commands my respect.... I would, however like the reciters to realize that the mere recitation is not an end in itself. It should be an aid to the contemplaton and assimilation of the meaning and the message of the Gita. By patience even a parrot can be taught to recite by heart. But it would be no wiser for the recitation. The reciter of the Gita should be what its author expects the reciter to be — a yogi in its broad sense. It demands from its votaries balance in every thought, word and deed and a perfect correspondence between the three. One whose speech and action do not accord with one's thoughts is a humbug or a hypocrite' (ibid., pp. 170-1).

'Devotion is not merely lip-worship: it is a wrestling with death....

'[It] is no soft-hearted effusiveness. It certainly is not blind faith. [It] has the least to do with externals. A devotee may use, if that devotee likes, rosaries and forehead marks or make offerings, but these things are no test of a devotee's devotion ....

'The popular notion of [devotion] is soft-heartedness, telling beads and the like and disdaining to do even a loving service lest the telling of beads might be interrupted. This [devotee] therefore leaves the rosary only for eating, drinking and the like, never for grinding corn or nursing patients.

'But the Gita says, "no one has attained one's goal without action..."' (ibid., pp. 160-1, paragraphs 9, 10, 13).

In Vrindavan Shri Krishnaprem saw a *vaishnava* dying of typhoid. All round, coming and going were *vaishavas* with rosaries in their hands, but there was no one to give this person even a glass of water. 'What can be the value of such worship as this?' he asked. See his **The Search for Truth**, p. 26.

SOURCES FOR QUOTES

[All quotes are Gandhi's, except as otherwise noted. Those not by him are documented in the text. Throughout the **Discourses,** Gandhi himself quotes Sir Edwin Arnold's English translation of the Gita, published under the title **The Song Celestial.**

Quote on page 4: **The Story of My Experiments With Truth** (Gandhi's Autobiography), Part IV, Chapter V.

First quote on page 5: **Harijan,** December 16, 1939, p. 382.

Second quote on page 5: **Young India,** August 6, 1925, p. 273.

Quote on page 6: **Harijan,** March 23, 1940, pp. 54-55.]